The ENNEAGRAM

for Recovery

The

ENNEAGRAM

for

Recovery

○

Expanded Spiritual Growth

Jenner K

H | Happy
D | Destiny
P | Publishing

Happy Destiny Publishing

First edition December 2020

Book design by Jenner K
        Figures and diagrams by Jenner K

Includes bibliographical references.
        The use of quoted material does not imply endorsement
        by the authors.

The Library of Congress Cataloging
        Jenner K
        The Enneagram for Recovery: Expanded Spiritual Growth

1. Enneagram 2. Spiritual growth 3. Twelve-step recovery 4. Psychology I. Title

ISBN: 978-0-578-82855-8

Published by Happy Destiny Publishing

To my beloved daughter and friends in the room(s)

TABLE OF CONTENTS

Identifying Our Shadow
Befriending the Shadow
Integrating the Shadow
Shadow Work

Living Amends
Minimizing Reactivity
Nonviolent Communication
Four Components of NVC
Needs Inventory
Feelings When Our Needs <u>Are</u> Satisfied
Feelings When Our Needs Are <u>Not</u> Satisfied

The Wings Offer Balance
Stronger Wing
Wing Types
The 18 Wing Types
Weaker Wing

Improve Our Contact
Balancing Across Centers
Body Work
Emotions Work
Meditations for Head Work
Unity

Our Past
Moving Forward
Forward-Arrow per Type

Your Type's Slogan
Recap of All Your Work
Ongoing Spiritual Growth Plan
Parting Thoughts

INTRODUCTION

If you're like me, I imagine that you have little patience for a long introduction about "Here's what I'm going to tell you." So let me cut to the point: the primary purpose of this book is to introduce the Enneagram's system of personal growth to the recovery community. We are spiritual seekers and are quick to see if this system is the right one for us. We already had our Egos cracked open when we faced our powerlessness over our addictions—and benefit from keeping our Egos low through continual spiritual growth. What this book offers is how to leverage the similarities between Twelve Step recovery and the Enneagram for an enlarged program of practical spirituality.

The Enneagram is a powerful psycho-spiritual study of nine unique personality types that shares many commonalities with the Twelve Step Program of recovery. Whether your addiction was drugs, alcohol, alcoholics, gambling, or something else, if you were like me, it brought you to the edge of ruin. This book is *not* meant for someone in his or her first time through the Steps. It's too important to not cloud priorities. As one of our long-time members says, "Alcoholic-addicts like to paint the burning house." I believe he is cautioning us against taking on too much too soon. So if you are in your first time through the Steps, trust the process of concentrating on Step work first, and you will gain so much added clarity that you will be ready for more spiritual growth. And if there's one word to encourage you toward spiritual growth, it's the word **MORE**—as in answer to "What were you addicted to?"—**MORE.**

I will often be quoting from *Alcoholics Anonymous*, informally known as the Big Book. You will find similar ideas in your individual Anonymous material. I will abbreviate our various programs as XA so you can fill in the X with your individual program.

I have found the Twelve Steps and the Enneagram complementary and not contradictory because the Twelve

Steps work from the **Outside-In** on our behaviors while the Enneagram works from the **Inside-Out** at our motivations. When we first enter recovery, we are told that "Why?" is not a spiritual question. The answer to how to proceed in recovery is "HOW," for Honest, Open-minded and Willing. This priority to work on behavior first is captured in the Big Book story "Crossing the River of Denial." The newly recovering alcoholic recounts,

> In fact I stopped wondering "Why me?" a long time ago. It's like a man standing on a bridge in the middle of the river with his pants on fire wondering why his pants are on fire. It doesn't matter. Just jump in![1]

After a few years, the fire *is* put out—we are creating much less wreckage and are ready to enrich our spiritual lives. Both the Twelve Step Program and the Enneagram say:

- The required psychic change happens both at the psychological and spiritual level.
- Only the individual can do the work.
- We don't do the work alone—we learn in groups and need our Higher Power, however we conceive of that.

What makes the Enneagram such a powerful spiritual tool is that rather than just describe our personality behaviors, as many other psychological typographies do, it works from the **Inside-Out** to really get at our unaddressed needs and what was driving our "full flight from reality." It makes sense that we will make the fastest progress if we can work from both directions: stop doing unhealthy behavior and figure out how to change what is driving it in the first place.

According to George I. Gurdjieff, who introduced the Enneagram from the Mideast to Paris and London in the 1920s, the spiritual life is not exclusive to hermits and recluses.[2] He acknowledged that one could obtain enlightenment through abnegation of the body as the fakirs practice. One could also train the emotions as the monks have done or seek enlightenment through the mind as the yogis have. But there is a way that combines body, emotion and the mind. This holistic approach was open to ordinary people living in their *everyday lives*. This practice he called the Fourth Way. Or as AA's cofounder Bill W phrased this practical spirituality in the Big Book,

> We have come to believe He would like us to keep our *heads in the clouds* with Him, but that our *feet ought to be firmly planted on earth*. That is where our fellow travelers are, and that is where our work must be done.[3]

I have been an active member of the recovery community since 1994 and am dedicated to that above everything else. I have studied the Enneagram since 1997, have attended workshops and participate in a few different Enneagram communities. The Enneagram, while in no way is a replacement for working the Steps, deepens my understanding and connection with myself, with my Higher Power and with others. We'll study the abbreviations used later, but I'll tell you now that my Enneagram Type is Type 5 with a SP/SX/SO Instinctual Sequence and a strong Type 4 Wing. I do not assert that I am an expert in this profound system. There are many comprehensive books and websites listed in the **Resources** section at the end to not duplicate effort.

Following is a short quiz to start to figure out your Type. I recommend also taking an online quiz to determine your Enneagram Type. There are free ones such as offered by EclecticEnergies or commercial ones from iEQ9 or RHETI. If you are undecided about your Type after taking a quiz, proceed with this workbook. There are questions at the end of every chapter to help clarify where you are and where you are headed. You will find your Type as you begin to apply these principles to your own life. Uncovering our best selves is the work of a lifetime. You may choose to work the suggestions in the questions more slowly or you may do a quick once-over and work them again with a friend or group.

??? Questions

1. What is your Enneagram Type?

2. How closely aligned do you feel to this Type?

3. Personal growth involves **Awareness** of what's not working; **Acceptance** that when we try on the new behavior, we're likely to overshoot the mark or do the new behavior awkwardly at first, and finally **Action**—putting new behaviors into day-to-day practice and modifying them once we see how they work. Are you in a place in your life to deal with this awkwardness and being out of your comfort zone?

Enneagram Quiz

Check all that sound particularly true for you, tally the totals per Type, and that is your likely Type. You will want to confirm this by taking a commercially available Enneagram test with many years of validated research behind it, especially to decide between two or more Types.

TYPE 1

_____ 1. Even as a child, I wondered why people couldn't keep their commitments and be more reliable.

_____ 2. Some of my best traits are that I have integrity, am honest and responsible.

_____ 3. I get frustrated with all the flaws I see in me and the world.

_____ 4. Justice—in my small sphere or to the societal level— is important to me.

_____ 5. When people call me a perfectionist, I take it as a compliment because I am one.

_____ 6. I have a hard time relaxing, taking it easy and being spontaneous.

_____ 7. I have acted the good boy or girl but sometimes get tired of it.

_____ 8. I have got into trouble telling others what to do.

_____ 9. Would I rather be right or happy? Well, I'm happy when I'm right.

_____10. I need to be seen as good and true.

TYPE 2

_____ 1. As a child, I could see what people needed, and I felt good about helping them.

_____ 2. I value my emotional intelligence and ability to give support to others.

_____ 3. I get frustrated when I take time to figure out others' needs, and they don't for me.

_____ 4. If I had to choose between getting a project done or not stepping on people's toes, I'd choose what's best for people.

_____ 5. I can get co-dependently involved in loved ones' lives.

_____ 6. It's hard for me to advocate and speak up for myself.

_____ 7. I compliment others a lot and worry if they would still like me if I didn't.

_____ 8. I have sometimes shared too much at work and have a hard time turning off my feelings.

_____ 9. Not only is the glass half full, but I generally have enough to share.

_____10. I need to be appreciated and loved.

TYPE 3

_____ 1. As a child, I dreamed of being a star in my field—I loved the attention!

_____ 2. Some of my best traits are that I am competent and will get the job done with style.

_____ 3. I don't have time for wishy-washy people who take forever to act.

_____ 4. Being seen as successful and knowing influential people is important to me.

_____ 5. I can size up what motivates people and change my behavior in response.

_____ 6. I don't like being around people who raise my fear level.

_____ 7. When I don't know how to show my feelings, I can appear cold and even superior.

_____ 8. I stay away from many emotional commitments and have a history of moving on.

_____ 9. If I had to choose between getting a project done or not stepping on people's toes, well, those people shouldn't have their toes on my runway.

_____10. I'd love to be loved for simply who I am, not what I do.

TYPE 4

_____ 1. As a child, I could get lost in my own world of fantasy and make-believe.

_____ 2. My unique gifts are being able to go to the deep side and see the beauty there.

_____ 3. I want to be seen for who I really am.

_____ 4. I often compare myself to others to figure out if I'm better-than or worse-than.

_____ 5. Being true to my emotions is important, and I dislike it when others seem emotionally inauthentic.

_____ 6. I don't like a lot of structure imposed on me, but it's good when I choose it.

_____ 7. I tend to have very few close friends, as most people don't really understand me.

_____ 8. I can feel other people's feelings so strongly that it can feel like a burden.

_____ 9. I idealize what I don't have and see the grass as greener someplace else.

_____10. I need to be thought of as special, just to feel all right.

TYPE 5

_____ 1. When I was a child, I could get lost in what interested me.

_____ 2. Some of my best traits are that I am intellectually curious, can put together seemingly different ideas and am competent.

_____ 3. I don't like stupidity and inefficient bureaucracies.

_____ 4. Going deeply into what I'm studying and understanding is important to me.

_____ 5. I'd rather be a lone contributor than have people tell me what to do.

_____ 6. I try not to act on impulse and have a hard time being spontaneous.

_____ 7. I minimize my needs so that I won't feel let down.

_____ 8. I am conscious of my energy level and get nervous when I feel it's being depleted.

_____ 9. I don't live in an ivory tower. Where's that drawbridge?!

_____10. I'd like to know that what I ask for isn't too much so I could open up.

Type 6

_____ 1. As a child, I was extra fearful—and still am, although I try to hide it.

_____ 2. Some of my best traits include my loyalty, dependability and being down to earth.

_____ 3. I get frustrated when others don't follow the rules when I do (usually).

_____ 4. I may test to see if you're trustworthy, and then I'll defend you until the end.

_____ 5. I can be very skeptical of authority *or* want the structure of authority.

_____ 6. I have a hard time relaxing and need to get into my body for some peace of mind.

_____ 7. I like to run a decision past a few people before acting.

_____ 8. I have a great sense of responsibility.

_____ 9. I'm not a disaster prepper. Everyone needs fifteen cases of water.

_____10. I need to feel safe and secure.

Type 7

_____ 1. As a child, I invented new ways to have fun and got friends to go along.

_____ 2. I love my enthusiasm and optimism for life.

_____ 3. I get frustrated with slow, traditional thinkers.

_____ 4. I need a lot of different stimulation to feel satisfied, and **MORE** is better.

_____ 5. I am a "big ideas" person; I like to start projects and don't like to get bogged down in the details.

_____ 6. I have a hard time quieting my mind, so things like meditation are hard.

_____ 7. I need my freedom and don't like to commit ahead unless I have to.

_____ 8. I am good at networking to help others and especially if it helps me.

_____ 9. I am outspoken, speak my mind and my feelings, and if others don't like, oh well . . .

_____10. I want to feel that my spiritual hole is finally getting filled.

Type 8

_____ 1. As a child, I had a strong personality that I could use to charm people or stop them from messing with me.

_____ 2. I think my strengths are that I can motivate others, get things done and am very straightforward.

_____ 3. I know when someone is lying to me and can't stand it if someone tries to manipulate me.

_____ 4. I like it when I'm the one in charge and can use my authority to make a difference.

_____ 5. I prefer to teach people to help themselves instead of rescuing them.

_____ 6. It's hard for me to let down my guard and be vulnerable—only my closest people know that I have a heart of gold.

_____ 7. I can sense who has the power in the room and make sure I get my share of it.

_____ 8. I think I've looked for a fight even when I didn't have to.

_____ 9. I understand the sign that reads, "If you love something, set it free. If it doesn't come back, hunt it down and kill it."

_____10. I need to feel in charge of my own life.

Type 9

_____ 1. As a child, I was often the mediator in my family—I couldn't stand to see people argue or feel conflict in the air.

_____ 2. I believe I'm a humble person (if you can say that without making it untrue) and have a calming force on those around me.

_____ 3. I'm usually kind to people, and not for any praise but for my own peace of mind.

_____ 4. I can get busy with everything except what matters most to me.

_____ 5. I don't like a lot of high stress and people pushing me to do things.

_____ 6. I don't like to show off but just to get the job done.

_____ 7. I tend to be idealistic about the world and past relationships.

_____ 8. I've always been a seeker and thrive on new ideas and things to keep me going.

_____ 9. If someone asks me to do something I don't want to do, I'll get around to it . . . . eventually.

_____ 10. I need to hear that I am visible—that what I want matters, and that I matter.

CHAPTER 1

EGO ADDICTION: Naming the Problem

STEP 1
***We admitted we were powerless over [X]–
that our lives had become unmanageable.***

People who are driven by pride of self unconsciously blind themselves to their liabilities. . . . The problem is to help them discover a chink in the walls their ego has built, through which the light of reason can shine.[1]

—*Twelve Steps and Twelve Traditions*

We are all spiritually powerless, however, and not just those physically addicted to a substance . . . Alcoholics just have their powerlessness visible for all to see. The rest of us disguise it in different ways, and overcompensate for our more hidden and subtle addictions and attachments, especially our addiction to our way of *thinking*.[2]

—Richard Rohr, *Breathing Under Water*

What is the Enneagram?

The Enneagram combines a psychological typology of nine different personality types with a spiritual dimension for growth. The name Enneagram comes from *ennea-* (Greek for nine) and *-gram* (Greek for drawing), depicted in the nine-sided figure below. Basic personality Types and their defects have been recognized for thousands of years. Evagrius Ponticus called them the Eight Evil Thoughts in the 4th Century, pared down to the Seven Deadly Sins by Pope Gregory I in the 6th Century,[3] and then expanded to our current understanding of Nine Passions by Bolivian Oscar Ichazo in the 1960s.[4] The low side of compulsive behaviors is called the Passions when the Feeling center is out of alignment with the high side of our Virtues. Likewise, our low side of perception is called the Fixations when our Thinking center is out of alignment with our Holy Ideas.

The other half of what the psycho-spiritual Enneagram studies is our psychology. Psychology is the study of our mental-emotional states and behavior and reflects our coping strategy with the world. This world view solidifies early and can be seen as armor protecting our undifferentiated Essence or soul. Our Essence gets covered up with a dominant coping strategy around the Body (Instinctual)—Head (Thinking)—Heart (Feeling) centers centering on Types 9-6-3, respectively. Types 2, 3 and 4 focus on their Feelings; Types 5, 6 and 7 with their Thinking and Types 8, 9 and 1 with their Instincts. We have all nine personality Types in us but develop our Ego around inhabiting one particular Type. To be sure, our Type within the Body-Head or Heart center gives us our strengths, but at the price of being not as strong and comfortable with the other centers.

The circle encompassing the Enneagram figure represents Oneness or Wholeness, as it does in the recovery symbol. The 9-6-3 triangle represents holy trinities found in many spiritual traditions. The hexagon's 1-4-2-8-5-7 order is obtained by dividing 1 by 7 = 0.142857, a repeating decimal.

We will study the significance of the order of numbers later when we examine spiritual growth using the arrows.

Centers of Intelligence

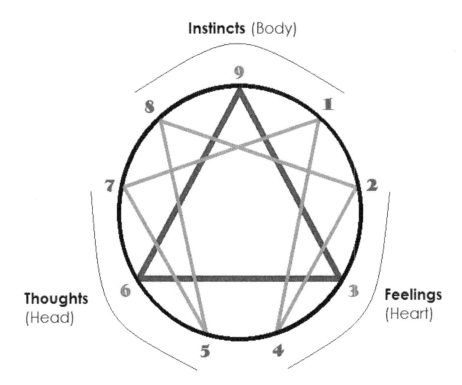

Common Questions

Let's clear up misconceptions. Some common questions people have about the Enneagram are:

> **?** How set is my personality Type? Maybe I was in extra fear today and tested as a Type 6, but tomorrow I'll be something else? — No, your personality Type is stable if you have taken a reliable test. We have access to many different personality traits coming from all nine Enneagram Types, but we always come back to our home Type.

> **?** The symbol looks pretty mystical, even astrological. This isn't a cult or strange religion? — No, it's not a religion or anything like that. It's a spiritual-psychological system with an ancient symbol.

> **?** I've taken the Myers-Briggs test and a couple of other personality tests. How related are they to the Enneagram? — Some personality tests are purely descriptive. They are useful for career counseling and better self-knowledge. The Myers-Briggs test is multi-layered and has some overlap with the Enneagram, but similarities won't be analyzed here. The Enneagram is unique for offering clear directions for spiritual and psychological growth using the arrow lines that we'll study.

> **?** Can the Enneagram be used to predict compatibility, especially for choosing a partner? — The Enneagram says that all different Types are compatible, provided that the people are functioning at their higher levels. And the reverse is true too. People of the same Type could be disastrous together if they haven't done spiritual work and are operating out of the lower levels of Ego.

Personality Type as Addiction

Bill W hit bottom and found sobriety in 1934, and then struggled more than a dozen years with depression. Despite having his sudden and spectacular spiritual awakening, despite his co-founding AA that Henry Kissinger dubbed the "greatest accomplishment of the 20th century," despite his tireless service helping others, and despite taking long walks that he knew relieved his depression for a short while—he had depression. He hit a second bottom of powerlessness over his own Ego demands, his whole approach to life. Bill W was reportedly a Type 3 and it was this commitment to excellence and achievement that made founding an international program of recovery possible. But it wasn't until he could break his faulty ego dependencies for prestige, so characteristic of Type 3, that his depression lifted. He wrote:

> My basic flaw had always been dependence—almost absolute dependence—on people or circumstances to supply me with prestige, security and the like. Failing to get these things according to my perfectionist dreams and specifications, I had fought for them, and when defeat came, so did my depression. There wasn't a chance of making the outgoing love of St. Francis a workable and joyous way of life until these fatal and almost absolute dependencies were cut away.[5]

Not all people hit such a severe bottom in Ego addiction as Bill W, but facing our ego's limitations can free all of us. As Fr Richard Rohr put it in the quotation at the beginning, we all have an "addiction to our way of *thinking*." Some people avoid personality typing as "putting people in a box" or seeming too restrictive. Far from being a reductive system to limit ourselves, the study of the Enneagram actually opens doors. It exposes how our thinking—our very way of being—is only one-ninth of the full picture of reality. It's been said that we have to *have* an Ego before we can *lose* our Ego. The Enneagram first describes our Ego traps and then provides a personalized roadmap for the way out. It shows how to stop over-using our defects, known as Passions in the Enneagram community, and uncover our Essential qualities, known as our Virtues.

We could approach understanding our personality superficially in a "magazine quiz of the month" way. We could read pages of ego-satisfying traits we have and gain a bit of awareness but not enough depth to engender real change. Then there's another trap we could fall in— doing spiritual, psychological work—but mechanically. I know when I was newly in recovery, I was a good little student. I did the readings and took the suggestions without necessarily feeling them at first. That's what I needed to outrun the return of my Ego. But more is required now. As Bill W put it, we don't have to be saints by Thursday, but we *do* need to maintain our spiritual growth. We will be challenging what the Ego has taken so long to build. It is recommended that we start spiritual work s-l-o-w-l-y. We can expect some back-sliding as we try on new behaviors and new ways of thinking and feeling.

Underlying Motivations

What sets the Enneagram system for personal growth apart from mere psychological typing of behaviors is that the Enneagram gets to our underlying motivations. For example, people who are Type 2 and Type 9 are generally nice, kind people. So while their behavior appears similar, Type 2s are looking for recognition for their kindness while Type 9s behave kindly to buy their own peace of mind. Likewise, Types 1, 3 and 5 share a behavioral value of competence, but Type 1 people would seek competence because it's "right," Type 3s to gain status or recognition, and Type 5s to prove they have mastered some field of study.

So be careful of typing people in your head because we don't know their underlying motivations. The Enneagram provides so much insight that it's tempting to type our friends (or our foes) to understand and get along with them. Like it was in identifying as an addict/alcoholic/gambler/whatever, it's better to let people make up their own minds. This really is fun and opens up whole new worlds— but it's not useful to put *others* in a box.

Awareness—Acceptance—Action
As people in recovery, we are already well aware of the "personality change at depth" process. We will use the same practice in uncovering our Essential selves:
Awareness—Acceptance—Action

We start with Awareness of where we truly stand now, a fair appraisal of our good and not so good coping traits. This awareness has to be done with as much non-condemning presence as possible. As one friend puts it when she sees herself slide back into old patterns, "Do you see God what I'm up to again?" This she does with a smile on her face because she recognizes her humanity with humility. Using our inner critic to shame us into better ways of seeing and behaving was like using willpower to try to overcome our addiction—it just sprang up sideways. Instead of the critic, we need to cultivate our inner observer. With practice, we'll get better at that spot-check inventory in the middle of the day while our Egos are acting up.

The Acceptance stage is similarly done with a combination of compassion and dedication to go toward better things. It requires open-mindedness because while our old way of reacting wasn't all bad, we see it now as limiting. Acceptance might entail getting in touch with sadness over time misspent or grief in saying goodbye to our former selves.

Action means actually trying on new behaviors, mentally and emotionally switching places with the people we dislike, doing more of what we do too little of (shortcomings) and less of what we do too much of (defects). Action requires noticing the effect our actions have on others and checking in with our Higher Power (HP). As we get feedback from our actions' effect, we can modify our choices and start the Awareness—Acceptance—Action cycle over again. If we maintain presence in our own bodies, our own breath, and the realization that we have a Higher Power, all will be well.

Psychologist Nathaniel Branden summarized the process of psychological growth well:

> The person who accepts himself, whatever his real or imagined shortcomings, is capable of moving from self-awareness to the attainment of new understanding and new integrations, to the attainment of a superior manner of being and of functioning. The man who repudiates himself is not; he has no base from which to move.[6]

Principles per Step

This list of Principles per Step, while not part of our conference-approved literature, has helped members since Rita L first introduced it at the 2003 General Service Conference of AA.[7] They are short and sweet and help us condense large ideas to "practice these principles in all our affairs."

Step	Principle
1	Honesty
2	Hope
3	Faith
4	Courage
5	Integrity
6	Willingness
7	Humility
8	Compassion
9	Balance or Justice
10	Perseverance
11	Spirituality
12	Service

Type	Virtue
1	Serenity
2	Humility
3	Veracity
4	Equanimity
5	Nonattachment
6	Courage
7	Sobriety
8	Innocence
9	Right Action

Notice how many of our Twelve Step Principles share similarities with the Enneagram Virtues: Honesty is another word for Veracity; Courage and Humility have the same names as in the Enneagram, and Balance has a lot in common with Equanimity. Principles or Virtues are everlasting—they provide a light in the storm. They help us weather true tragedies of loss of loved ones, work or relationship upsets and illness. Because they are ideals, they are bigger than any of us and will survive long after we're gone. And as ideals, we may never fully reach them but can gain a more soulful life by demonstrating them in our everyday lives. So post your own Type's Virtue where you can see it in the morning and use it as your guiding light throughout your day.

Can't Get Out of This Alone

The chapter "We Agnostics" in the Big Book reminds us:

> We could wish to be moral, we could wish to be philosophically comforted, in fact, we could will these things with all our might, but the needed power wasn't there. Our human resources, as marshaled by the will, were not sufficient; they failed utterly. Lack of power, that was our dilemma. We had to find a power by which we could live, and it had to be a *Power greater than ourselves*. Obviously.[8]

Our spiritual growth spurt is likely to follow the same process that worked in early recovery. At first, we borrow hope from others and copy their behavior. We can avail ourselves of outside support in the form of Enneagram workshops, online events and an abundant number of books (see the **Resources** section at the back).

But during this spiritual journey, there will likely come a time when it is between you and your Higher Power. We can do the self-awareness exercises; we can chart progress in practicing new behaviors; we can openly share with a therapist, if desired, on family dynamics that still plague us; we can do-do-do and yet there comes a time for grace. We sit patiently and allow our HP to do for us "what we could not do for ourselves."[9]

It is good to solidify why you want spiritual growth and what you're hoping to get. My answer to why not pat myself on the stomach and reach for the remote control was that I felt the meaning in my life could slip away. I want to make the most of the time I have here. I want to live the best version of my life and not let my reoccurring patterns of Ego block me. I want to be of real service to my Higher Power, myself and those around me. Simply stated:

My Spiritual Goal—To lead my biggest life possible.

??? Questions

1. What is your Spiritual Goal?

2. What were some of the reasons that drinking/using/ compulsive behaviors were so attractive? This is not the old alibis and excuses we made up before entering recovery. What were you needing to *avoid* or needing *to get* through using?

3. What are your top three thinking or behavioral ruts you'd like to escape?

CHAPTER 2

OUR ENNEAGRAM TYPE: Possible Solution

STEP 2
Came to believe that a Power greater than ourselves could restore us to sanity.

It is easy to let up on the spiritual program of action and rest on our laurels. . . . What we really have is a daily reprieve contingent on the maintenance of our spiritual condition.[1]

—*Alcoholics Anonymous*

We all become addicted to an egocentric, self-serving style of living that we've come to believe is not only normal but also good. Having entered this cycle of egocentricity, we have created disharmony within ourselves and in the world. Until we begin to recognize how this imbalance has created layers and layers of illusion that distort our perception of reality, the cycle will continue, because we see nothing wrong with our perceptions.[2]

—Kathleen Hurley, *My Best Self*

Possible Paths

The internal arrow lines of the Enneagram depict arrows to other Types for growth. It makes sense that people who share personality traits will benefit most from adopting and adding a unique set of traits compared to people sharing different traits. For example, people who already display plenty of aggression would need to soften while people-pleasers need to find their own inner guidance and strength. When the Enneagram was introduced to the general public in the 1980s, it was taught that there was a single path preferred for spiritual growth. The Virtues from our Back-Arrow Type were contrasted with the Passions or defects from our Forward-Arrow Type. Of course, the Type representing our Forward-Arrow suffered in comparison. All Types have a high and a low functioning side. Each Type has many splendid qualities that people from that Type bring to the world. But when we are spiritually off-center, we act out the low-side of behaviors from that Type.

It is more commonly thought now that we can grow by integrating the Virtues from both of our arrows. Let's look at the Enneagram figure to see how this works.

The Enneagram of the Virtues

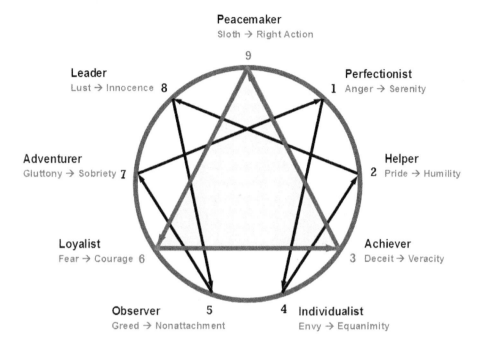

Peacemaker
Sloth → Right Action
9

Leader
Lust → Innocence 8

Perfectionist
1 Anger → Serenity

Adventurer
Gluttony → Sobriety 7

Helper
2 Pride → Humility

Loyalist
Fear → Courage 6

Achiever
3 Deceit → Veracity

Observer 5
Greed → Nonattachment

4 Individualist
Envy → Equanimity

The Enneagram Approach

The process of spiritual growth is multi-stepped and can sound complex. As the Twelve Steps are in order for a reason, there is a recommended order of integrating new motivations and behavior into our "home" Enneagram Type. Yes, we have traits from all nine Types, but we'll make the fastest progress if we focus on our home Type first instead of paying attention to all Types' Ego pitfalls. Then we try on the behavior from our Back-Arrow Type. We are apt to do that awkwardly for a while, and then feel our world expand a good deal. We're becoming more of the person we were meant to be.

When our Ego flares up, demanding that we go back to the good old days when we could live on autopilot, we might take a detour and work on access to our Wing Types. Our Wings are the Types adjacent to our Type around the circle, not along the arrows. So Wings of Type 1 are 9 and 2; for Type 2 are 1 and 3, etc. The Wings were thought to account for the variability seen between people of the same Type. While Wings give us access to more behavioral tools and therefore support, variability within Type has been supplanted more recently with the Instincts. Don't worry—we'll study the Instincts later and their huge impact on behavior and Essence.

Finally, after living more days in the solution of the Virtues, we can challenge ourselves and borrow behaviors from our Forward-Arrow Type. Again, we are likely to do that awkwardly at first. For example, as a Type 5, I could be having a good day, displaying all my glowing 5 traits along with my Back-Arrow behaviors of Type 8 and my Forward-Arrow behaviors of Type 7. But on a spiritually-off day, those same traits from Types 5, 8 and 7 would look very different.

This may be sounding complicated, but exposing you now to all of the avenues open to growth gives you the big picture. It's like seeing the Twelve Steps on the wall, "What an order! I can't go through with it."[3] Then we are shown how and DO go through with it.

We are constantly looping back to our home Type but now have added four other Types' Virtues. We add not only the behaviors but the underlying motivations from other Types, while keeping our Type as our home. By the end of extended practice, we will have expanded our view of the world from a one-ninth sliver to a healthy five-ninths piece of the pie. **MORE** is better.

What are the Passions and Virtues?
To cut to it, Passions are a euphemism for our defects. They are our Ego's compulsive stranglehold to proclaim that our way is right, and others are misdirected. Passions are the way we lose sight of our Virtues because we're afraid that the universe won't deliver what we want. We don't need to defend something so vigorously unless under all that bluster is the sneaking suspicion that another route might be better. The Passions are fueled by our Feelings and will need to be

redirected gently at first. We have spent decades building this protection, and we will likely need our Higher Power's help to let go.

We were exposed to the Passions in the form of the Seven Deadly Sins when doing our 4th Step inventory in recovery. The Enneagram adds Deceit for Type 3 and Fear for Type 6, and both of those Passions receive plenty of coverage in our literature. In our Enneagram work, we will first focus on the Passion and Virtue just of our Type. It may not seem at first that your Passion is the #1 problem. I always assumed Pride (Type 2's) was my #1 downfall. But it was Pride in my intellect, and therefore Greed (Type 5's) at hoarding vital information that was creating problems. There is a fish-in-water phenomenon of not seeing how our particular Passion manifests in our life.

Virtues are us approaching our Essence. We not only behave but underneath think and feel no irreparable wrong done to us. Sure, life offers many knocks—but to borrow the Virtue of Equanimity from Type 4, we come back to center and don't live for years in resentment. It is much easier to let go of old coping strategies when we go toward new ones. Sobriety, Serenity and Courage are lights on the near horizon.

What the Passions and Virtues Look Like

By now, you should have taken one of the Enneagram quizzes listed in the Introduction and found your Type. You may have read the healthy and not so healthy traits associated with your Type. These not so healthy Passions are named for the Seven Deadly Sins of Pride, Anger, Greed, Gluttony, Lust, Envy and Sloth (a useful mnemonic is PAGGLES), plus Deceit and Fear. There is no religious or moral failing implied here. These shortcomings represent major categories of human failing across the ages. Here is a slightly tongue-in-cheek take on what the Types can look like in meetings for everyday examples before we look at them more closely.

Type	The High and Low Side of Behavior
1	They know and protect the Traditions. They rewrite the format as soon as they become secretary to make it "better."
2	They bake the cookies and thank everyone who participated. They get their feelings hurt if no one thanks them.
3	They work hard to get good, influential speakers for the meeting. They want others to conform to their superior way of doing things.
4	They eloquently put their emotions into words. They stew about the fluorescent lights or ramp up talking about emotions for others to hear them.
5	They know the history and lesser-known facts about the program. They get in a snit if others don't acknowledge their intellectual contributions.
6	They share in a practical salt-of-the-earth way. They can sound authoritarian or anti-authoritarian about the doctrine of the program.
7	These are the fun and funny members who lighten things up. They can seem like they're skirting on the surface or are self-absorbed.
8	They are clear and direct and help organize the group. They can be loud and take over business meetings.
9	They get along with almost everyone, and everyone likes them. They can be wishy-washy at business meetings, so you don't know where they stand.

Passions to Virtues per Type

Many of the Passions need to be understood in ways different from their everyday usage. Type 7s may see Gluttony and think, "I watch my diet." Gluttony, as the Enneagram interprets it, is a preoccupation with the next pleasurable thing instead of concentrating on what's in front of them. And some of the Passions sound extreme and, well, biblical. Recall from *Twelve Steps and Twelve Traditions* (12&12), "But when we face up to the less violent aspects of these very same defects, then where do we stand?"[4] The Enneagram helps us root out subtle but pervasive patterns that have been holding us back. To understand the Passions and to remove any religious sting, here are common manifestations of the Passions and the healthy Virtues that are also ours.

~~~~~~

TYPE 1: "Perfectionist" Anger → Serenity

Passion: Anger- There is nothing wrong with our primary emotion of anger—that quick burst of adrenaline is to keep us safe. But *preparing* to see what's wrong in yourself and others, and rehashing in Resentment (your mental Fixation) is your Ego. It's black and white thinking wherein your way is the "right way"; it's judgementalism, moral superiority and rigid plans.

Virtue: Serenity- Aaah, keeping your moral compass but with compassion for yourself and others; openness, welcoming new ways of doing things; no need to keep score; playfulness.

TYPE 2: "Helper" Pride → Humility

Passion: Pride- If you don't do the job—it won't get done; needing others to rely on and appreciate you; giving with the hope that others will see what you need without asking.

Virtue: Humility- Your Higher Power has the plan; it's taking responsibility for your own needs; asking for help and giving without strings out of pure joy.

TYPE 3: "Achiever" Deceit → Veracity

Passion: Deceit- It's self-dishonesty; changing to fit in by adopting the style of different groups to gain recognition. It's needing to be seen as exceptional to feel good enough; seeking the limelight; impatience; using work to cover emotions and losing sight of who you are.

Virtue: Veracity- It's developing an unshakable foundation for life, with self-integrity; opening up to the power of

Feelings; doing without needing recognition—being more patient with less to prove.

TYPE 4: "Individualist"   Envy → Equanimity

Passion: Envy- It's seeing what others have as more desirable than what you have; nostalgia for better times in the past; needing to be unique to feel valued; comparing your insides to others' outsides.

Virtue: Equanimity- It's feeling yourself in the middle, not better or worse; savoring what you have; knowing who you are with a calmness of heart; not needing to prove any specialness; expanding your creativity to help others; living in the world as it is; enjoying beauty without hiding in sadness. Equanimity means having an "even mind," and being in balance.

TYPE 5: "Observer"   Greed/Avarice → Nonattachment

Passion: Greed- It's protecting your space and time against invasion from others; living minimalistically or not asking for help to not be let down or beholden; needing to be thought of as smart to be validated. It's a closed system that scans for what's coming in before giving.

Virtue: Nonattachment- It's letting things come and letting them go; trusting that your needs are important and will be met; not withdrawing into your mind; less control and more spontaneity.

TYPE 6: "Loyalist"   Fear → Courage

Passion: Fear- As with anger, primary fear is an honest emotion we all need in the moment. But planning ahead for any contingency; False Evidence Appearing Real (FEAR); overly dependent or overly suspicious of authority instead of acting out of your own agency; holding anxiety in your body and expecting the worse are from the Ego.

Virtue: Courage- It's Faith that you are secure and can get support as well as give it; finding a calm place of rest in your mind; going off-plan; walking through real fear.

TYPE 7: "Adventurer" Gluttony → Sobriety (Yay!)

Passion: Gluttony- It's being lured by the next temptation at the banquet of life; being restless and afraid of boredom; needing external stimuli to run from pain in search of pleasure; self-absorption out of disbelief you will be taken care of and living in the future.

Virtue: Sobriety- It's knowing that what you have is enough; perpetual calmness of mind (I see you nodding off . . .), persistence amid the mundane and knowing that you are being taken care of.

TYPE 8: "Leader" Lust → Innocence

Passion: Lust- It's power and intensity in all areas of life; overt aggression to get what you want; the need to be viewed as alpha; looking for betrayal or to prove your strength when there is no real challenge. On low days it's going out looking for a fight.

Virtue: Innocence- It's starting each encounter fresh, knowing that you are strong and no longer needing to prove it, letting down your guard and showing vulnerability to loved ones.

TYPE 9: "Peacemaker" Sloth → Right Action

Passion: Sloth- It's doing everything besides what you value as most important; going along with others to get along; losing sight of your own needs; taking comfort in narcotizing or obsessive behaviors that don't really soothe.

Virtue: Right Action- It's developing your own criteria for what is important and doing it; staying present in your body; trusting your right to be as you are.

~~~~~~

??? Questions

(Note: How long you spend observing each of these exercises is up to you. You may take longer or choose to move quickly the first time and revisit the questions again—alone or with a group.)

1. Does your particular Type's Passion and Virtue seem the most important one to work on to you? Even if other work calls to you, are you able to focus on your own Type's for now?

2. Looking back at the **Passions to Virtues per Type**, how much time are you acting out of the Virtue, and how much time are you stuck in the Passion?

3. Keep a notebook on you as you go through your day and record all of the manifestations of your Type's Passion. Can you begin to spot your coping mechanisms? You can also note when you are living out your healthy Virtue.

CHAPTER 3

Our Back-Arrow: What are we going to DO about it?

STEP 3
Made a decision to turn our will and our lives
over to the care of God <u>as we understood Him</u>.

So our troubles, we think, are basically of our own making. They arise out of ourselves, and the alcoholic is an extreme example of self-will run riot, though he usually doesn't think so.[1]

—*Alcoholics Anonymous*

Personality is limited in its ability to act in the world and can only grow to a point. When you can see this, you can initiate an effective program of personal development. When you can challenge the Personality's control, you begin the process of building up a conscious center of gravity within you that is the nucleus of your higher or "greater" or essential Self.[2]

—Beatrice Chestnut, *The Complete Enneagram*

Start Where You Are

In the first two chapters, we identified our fixed Ego patterns of how we see the world and behave. We observed ourselves repeating old patterns in our Passions and hopefully saw us practicing our own unique Virtues. This work can deepen over the coming months. What was not objectionable before suddenly comes to light as a limiting belief or feeling. Good! We won't move forward until we can see some benefit of a wider range of perceptions and behaviors.

Perhaps in this observation stage, you couldn't really grasp what the problem was. It's like the story in the Big Book of the farmer who claimed that physical sobriety was enough and said after the tornado, "Don't see anything the matter here, Ma. Ain't it grand the wind stopped blowin'?"[3] Sometimes this not-seeing isn't from denial so much as the fish-in-water phenomena of not seeing what we've become accustomed to. Another roadblock to change is Fear: fear of the unknown, fear of laying down one's defenses and being vulnerable, previous attempts to grow out of personality that didn't go well . . .

That's why finding the structure that the Enneagram provides is reassuring. Multitudes of people sharing the same personality Type found that trying on a particular set of new behaviors was the most efficient way to grow spiritually. This focused approach offers a shortcut to give us positive feedback to keep growing. It focuses our attention and effort in one direction at a time before we integrate all the new ways of seeing the world and being.

Proceed By Going Back a Step

Maybe some time in working the Steps, you came to one that you didn't know how to take. A wise sponsor may have suggested backing up a Step to make sure you were on firm ground before proceeding. Overcoming personality fixation is done much the same way. We have mixed success playing our same old patterns but don't know where to go from here. We all have unmet needs, unacknowledged issues and unaddressed problems left over from childhood. The Enneagram teaches that an efficient way of expanding our repertoire is actually to go back a step to address them.

Recall the flow of numbers from Chapter 1: the 9-6-3 triangle and the 1-4-2-8-5-7 hexagon. Look at the Type preceding your Type on the Enneagram. You'll see your Back-Arrow Type below, also called the "energizing point."

The Arrows: Your Personal Roadmap

You might ask, why adopt those strange new behaviors? What this Type holds is a wealth of underused resources. You may have gravitated to using some of these traits—both the up-side Virtues and the down-side Passions. Now you can practice using more of your Back-Arrow behaviors consciously until you begin to see more of the Virtue and less of the Passion.

Type	Back-Arrow Type Integrate First	Forward-Arrow Type Integrate Later
1	7	4
2	4	8
3	6	9
4	1	2
5	8	7
6	9	3
7	5	1
8	2	5
9	3	6

Take a moment to re-read the motivations and behaviors from your Back-Arrow Type in Chapter 2. Does any of this sound like parts of you left behind in childhood and what you're trying to work on now? As a person in recovery who does spiritual work every day, you may already be moving past just your old behavior into adopting some of the behavior from your Back-Arrow Type. Do you find yourself unaccountably displaying some of these traits now? One of the benefits of shifting attention to your Back-Arrow is that rather than the fish-in-water phenomena, it's likely to feel like a fish-*out*-of-water.

~~~~~~

Back-Arrow per Type

Since these are coping strategies abandoned in youth, it isn't likely we'll get them right at first. We will need a lot of self-acceptance to practice, get it wrong and then feel when we're starting to get these new behaviors right. You can notice when the Passion or low-side of your Back-Arrow Type is operating because you might not feel like yourself temporarily. If you can make a conscious decision to really use and integrate the Virtue, you'll feel increased emotional sobriety—like you're growing into the person you were meant to be. Here is what integrating the Virtues of our Back-Arrow Type might look like per Type:

TYPE 1: Back-Arrow Type 7   Gluttony → Sobriety

Type 1s hold themselves extra accountable and tend to be rigid. Type 7s are anything but rigid and delight in spontaneity and enjoying themselves. This idea of letting go and enjoying yourself can seem scary and undesirable to Type 1s. In the days before recovery, letting your hair down may have ended in handcuffs. Trust that you're not that same person anymore and notice the Virtue: Sobriety. Healthy Type 7s have slowed down their mad dash at grabbing for every positive experience they see. Sobriety means weighing the consequences using our mental faculties, and Type 1s know how to do that well.

Back-Arrow Work: Try having fewer expectations on how things should look. Demonstrate to your family that you can be messy, spontaneous and fun too. If you start a project and it turns out to be not right for you, move on without completing it. I heard you gasp, but you have more to gain than lose.

TYPE 2: Back-Arrow Type 4   Envy → Equanimity
Type 2s and Type 4s are both in the Heart center, and both Types scan others' emotions. But Type 2s can do shape-shifting by adopting the likes and behaviors they think will get them love—while Type 4s are more self-referential—they're comparing themselves to others for their *own* self-worth. Getting in touch with your Back-Arrow will show you painful Envy of comparing your insides to someone else's outsides. But it will also introduce powerful emotional authenticity. The searching that Type 4s do outside themselves is to craft a strong sense of self. Healthy Type 4s have learned Equanimity and know that we all have equal stature in our HP's universe. They also take greater intuitive leaps than Type 2s, who tend to be more literal.

Back-Arrow Work: Get in touch with how you're feeling during interactions and check that your emotions are yours and not mirroring what the other person shows. Own your own needs more and take action to get them met directly. You probably already have a creative side, so indulge it—from woodworking to gardening—because it will help you take those intuitive leaps to bring your authentic self to the foreground.

TYPE 3: Back-Arrow Type 6   Fear → Courage
Type 3s don't like to slow down to figure out how they're feeling. They can regard emotions as a sticky bog but know in the back of their minds that they need to face them. Remember, Face Everything And Recover. A big part of your process of getting real is to examine fear for what it was meant to do—alert us to something gone wrong in the environment or within ourselves—and gain the calm that comes from walking through Fear to Courage. Type 3s can do

their own version of shape-shifting to win praise from others. They need more of healthy Type 6's down to earth quality.

Back-Arrow Work: Get in touch with your Fear. This will not be pleasant. You may see it in many of your interactions throughout the day. But Type 3s have the look-good part of life down. You're trading in a thin layer of bravado for a deeper sense of self. Type 6s know that everything will be all right in the end—and so can you. So show your flaws and insecurities around people you trust before displaying them to the wider world. Then you will be living in real Courage.

TYPE 4: Back-Arrow Type 1   Anger → Serenity
Type 4s are committed to being their true selves; they just aren't sure of who that is. Type 1's knowing who they are and where they stand is the "container" for all that Type 4s possess. The low side of Type 1 is Anger, and Type 4s, particularly SX4s (we'll cover Subtypes in Chapter 5), can display Anger well. It's probable that you will overdo this healthy emotion at first. You are not shooting for childish, reactive Anger but the slow, rooted kind that moves mountains. I have seen beautiful transformations of Type 4s when they plant their feet and take a stand. They stop introjecting by taking on the moods and feelings from everyone around them and say: "NO, This is who I am." Then they know Serenity.

Back-Arrow Work: Part of the "container" that Type 1 offers for Type 4 is a firm grounding in the outside world. So on your next walk, get into your Body more than your Feelings and report just the facts to yourself: "It is about 68°, and there are yellow roses." Your Feelings are your gift to the world, but developing your rational side will balance them in Equanimity. Make sure you aren't just *acting* sad or mad but check in with your deeper authentic self for emotional Serenity. You can use Anger to fight *for* yourself rather than against yourself.

TYPE 5: Back-Arrow Type 8   Lust → Innocence
Type 5s are great with thinking before acting but lose the strength that comes from their Body center. Type 8s Lust, or going after what they want from their Body center, represents the animalistic push-back that Type 5s need. They worry they lack the resources to cope with all the demands from the outside world and need Type 8's confidence. As with early experiments with Anger, early attempts with lusty going after needs will likely be overdone. It's very uncomfortable for self-contained Type 5s to admit Innocence and unguarded need, but they step into their bigger lives when they do.

Back-Arrow Work: Type 5s can be bossy and controlling in arenas where they're comfortable. But they likely suffer the backlash of recrimination after asking for what they want. Try a combination of your mental forte by affirming to yourself many times a day, "It's a given that I have needs" and get into some vigorous physical exercise. Once you know that you are strong, you can adopt the healthy Type 8 Innocence to go less defended into the world. Your Body is your ally, make friends with it.

TYPE 6: Back-Arrow Type 9   Sloth → Right Action
Type 6s have Fear as their middle name. Even counterphobic Type 6s are scanning the area for possible harm. Type 9s take things easy. They are in the Body center that's in the present instead of Type 6's Head center that's in the future. Healthy Type 9s know when it's time to act. As the pilot whose story "Grounded" appears in the Big Book said, "But one day and one thing at a time they were doable. So I did them."[4] Fear can look like Sloth when you're afraid to get into Right Action, but Right Action is doable . . . so do it.

Back-Arrow Work: Type 6s intuitively know they need to be in their bodies for sanity. The trick is to bring their great minds along with them in a Head-Body awareness. Type 6s are another rigid Type out of Fear of the future and need Type 9s faith that right now, everything is okay. So don't turn off your mind during your next walk. Let the consciousness of your Fear come up, and let the Instincts from your Body center reassure you you're more than capable of the next Right Action.

TYPE 7: Back-Arrow Type 5   Greed → Nonattachment
Type 7s can understand Greed, but they also have no trouble in letting things go. What could pass for Type 5's Virtue of Nonattachment can be just Type 7s ability to skate on the surface. Type 7s benefit from Type 5's ability to go within for a more profound appreciation of life. Type 7s are afraid that by putting down deep roots, they'll lose mobility to move onto the next thing. Nonattachment is a commitment to care about the people and things in our life <u>and</u> the ability to let them go.

Back-Arrow Work: Type 7s need to temper their natural extroversion with the rich rewards introverted Type 5s know. Spend less time going out to the world for **MORE** experiences and savor the ones you have. You have a keen mind, so let your interests deepen instead of broaden. And as open as you seem, you may actually be running from your Feeling side, so practice talking about your feelings more in your relationships.

TYPE 8: Back-Arrow Type 2   Pride → Humility
Type 8s would rather be respected by most people than loved, as Type 2s do. They have lost touch with their child-like Innocence and can reclaim it in Humility. What a healthy Type 2 models for the strong Type 8 is the ability to show vulnerability. Yes, Pride in Type 2 makes them want to be appreciated, but isn't that under the demand to be respected? People in recovery already had the wake-up call that they're not the center of the universe. Type 8s need Humility to be reawakened to this fact for their best spiritual growth.

Back-Arrow Work: Accept the fact that you also want to be loved. You have proven you can exert yourself in the world. As much as you take care of others—remember Humility to know that you also need tender-loving-care. Feelings have long been a sore spot, so find some techniques (see Chapter 7) to express them—you'll be stronger for it.

TYPE 9: Back-Arrow Type 3   Deceit → Veracity

Type 9's Passion of Sloth makes them question how much effect they can have on the world. They can tap into Type 3's answer: a lot! Introverted Type 9s can fake the extroversion that Type 3s have to determine that they *do* matter and can make a difference. Deceit turns into real Veracity once you try it and see the rewards. "Fake it 'til you make it" can overcome inertia and give you back being present in your body and your life.

Back-Arrow Work: The next time someone asks who made that fabulous contribution—step up! The next time you can't make up your mind on which fork to take in the road— take one. You don't find out what you want by sitting on the sidelines, so get fully in the game.

~~~~~~

??? Questions

1. As you did for your own home Type, keep a notebook and record all of the manifestations of your Back-Arrow Type's Passion and Virtue in your everyday life. Was it easier to spot your Back-Arrow Passion than your own Type's?

2. How did it feel when you acted out of your Back-Arrow Type? Remember that your Back-Arrow contains issues left over from childhood. The discomfort of actively choosing new behavior will, in time, be followed by a sense of ease.

3. After you feel more at ease with your expanded menu of personality reactions, spend a while longer recording your own Type and Back-Arrow Type of reactions. Do you see how they can combine to reinforce each other?

CHAPTER 4

The Instincts: Bringing Them into Balance

STEP 4
*Made a searching and fearless
moral inventory of ourselves.*

Yet these instincts, so necessary for our existence, often far exceed their proper functions. Powerfully, blindly, many times subtly, they drive us, dominate us, and insist upon ruling our lives.[1]

—*Twelve Steps and Twelve Traditions*

When our consciousness is identified with our personality, these drives [instincts] become motivated by the passions and are thus distorted. The freer we are of our ego identification, the more these drives are informed by the virtues and function in an undistorted way.[2]

—Sandra Maitri, *The Enneagram of
Passions and Virtues*

Instincts in Collision

So far, we've talked about how the Passions arising from our Feeling center can get us off the beam and how we can use the Virtues to get back on the beam. Even more fundamental for our basic survival are our Instincts. Our Instincts arise out of our Body center, from our reptilian or hindbrain. Next, developmentally, our Passions arise from our Feeling center concentrated in our limbic system, located in the middle of the cerebral hemispheres. Last to develop is the Fixations arising from our Thinking center of the prefrontal cortex in the forebrain.[3] In a fight-flight or freeze situation, our Instincts are activated first and much faster than Feelings or Thoughts. Because the Instincts are from our ancient reptilian hindbrain that is responsible for survival functions, we hold Instinctual needs the tightest—they are closer to our core:

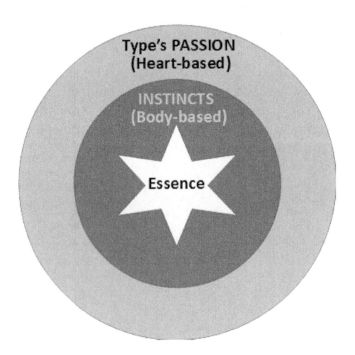

Eric Salmon, in *Subtypes: The Key to the Enneagram*, says that more misunderstandings stem from people operating from different dominant Instincts than from different personality Types.[4] In "How it Works" in the Big Book, it says that "we step on the toes of our fellows and they retaliate. Sometimes they hurt us, seemingly without provocation, but we invariably find that sometime in the past we have made decisions based on self which later placed us in a position to be hurt."[5] If one person with a low Social Instinct makes an off-hand comment regarding social status to someone with a Dominant Social Instinct, that person could take offense. None was intended by the Social Instinct Repressed person, and he or she could be wondering what the big deal was about.

Inventory of Our Instincts

The 4th Step inventory from the Big Book says, "Being convinced that self, manifested in various ways, was what had defeated us, we considered its common manifestations."[5] It then suggests an inventory of our resentments (our Social Instinct), our fears (our security or Self-Preservation Instinct) and our sex conduct (our Sexual Instinct). *Twelve Steps and Twelve Traditions* asks us directly to take an inventory of our social, security and sexual instincts. It affirms that the Instincts "so necessary for our existence, often far exceed their proper functions."

Think back to your fear inventory. Did most things you were afraid of affect your sex, security or social needs? That is probably your Dominant Instinct. Then there is an Instinct that you avoid dealing with in the world—that is your Repressed Instinct. The second most used Instinct, in what the Enneagram terms the "Instinctual Sequence," is the most balanced—neither overly-used nor repressed. Of course, we have all three Instincts, and the Secondary and Repressed Instincts can step to the front when needed. But when the situation has passed, our Instincts return to their baseline levels of preference.

What Are the Instincts?

The Instincts are powerful, Body-based forces. They represent the primal strategy of how best to survive. We all have a mixture of fight or flight strategies but, like the personality strategy of how best to get our needs met, we rely on one dominant survival Instinct over the others. The energy specific to the three Instincts can be summarized:

Instinct	Associated Energy
SP Self-Preservation	Withdrawing, Avoiding, Protecting
SX Sexual or One-to-One	Approaching, Acquiring, Fending off
SO Social	Connecting, Including, Relating

The Self Preservation Instinct is all about withdrawal. In caveman times, this is the person who would take what was hunted and gathered back to the cave to hoard it from others. These individuals are often more introverted and self-contained. They have a cooler energy since the primary strategy is self-survival—not investing one's survival in the group.

The Sexual Instinct is all about going toward the people we want and against others who could interfere. The Sexual Instinct Dominant caveperson would grab his or her mate and food away from others to bring back to the cave. These people are dynamic and display both an approaching-others and working-against energy. Their energy burns laser hot. Since their primary strategy is securing and taking care of their few important people, they might do so even if others get trampled along the way. Of course, in the boardroom, this will look more subtle than in the days of the caveman.

The Social Instinct is about connecting and merging with others. These social cavepersons are not the lone hermits up on the high cliffs. They are organizing the hunting-gathering parties because they believe their best chance of survival is within a group. They hand over some of their own autonomy and preferences to get along. Their energy is warm and all-encompassing.

Instinctual Sequence
The Instinctual Sequence, sometimes referred to as the stacking order, is the order of importance that we demand our Instinct be fulfilled. The most used Instinct is referred to as the Dominant Instinct, followed by the Secondary Instinct, followed by the Repressed Instinct, which requires nurturing. Each personality Type combines with one of the following Instinctual Sequences:

SP/SX/SO	SX/SP/SO	SO/SP/SX
SP/SO/SX	SX/SO/SP	SO/SX/SP

Where SP= The Self-Preservation or security need
SX= The Sexual or One-to-One relationship
SO= The Social Instinct

It's important to note that as we travel around the Enneagram acquiring traits from Back-Arrows, Wings and Forward-Arrow Types, we tend to take our preferred Instinctual Sequence with us. If you are a SO3 working on your Back-Arrow Type 6, you will likely be motivated and behave as a SO6. We will cover Subtypes in the next chapter. Now let's find out what your Dominant, Secondary and Repressed Instincts are.

Instincts Quiz
Check all that are vital to you, tally the totals per Instinct, and that is the likely Instinctual Sequence of your Dominant/Secondary/Repressed Instincts. But the way that Passions and Instincts combine can radically change how both appear, especially in Types 4 and 6.

Self-Preservation
_____ 1. I'd rather have a quiet evening at home than be out many times a week.
_____ 2. I make sure there's extra food in the pantry—you never know.
_____ 3. I can get anxious when my eating or sleeping times are interfered with.
_____ 4. I am a private person, and autonomy is important to me.
_____ 5. My home is my refuge, and I don't like uninvited guests.
_____ 6. It's important to me that loved ones understand my need for downtime.
_____ 7. I may not need much but like to take care of and protect what I have.
_____ 8. I protect my time and resource commitments.
_____ 9. I have many layers until you can get to know the real me.
_____10. I can get reactive around the high-energy or the social-butterfly type.

Sexual or One-to-One
_____ 1. I prefer good One-to-One conversations to a party any day.
_____ 2. I like intensity in my work, home and personal relationships.
_____ 3. Sexual chemistry is a top criterion in intimate relationships.
_____ 4. Some people are uncomfortable with the amount of eye contact I like.

_____ 5. When I walk into a room, I can immediately tell who can match my energy level.

_____ 6. It's important to me that an intimate partner stays faithful unless we both choose.

_____ 7. If I have to choose between being predator or prey—count me as the predator.

_____ 8. I'm not actively flirting—it's just what makes conversations come alive.

_____ 9. If someone messes with my family, there's going to be a problem.

_____10. I can get reactive around the drab-boring or the social-butterfly type.

Social

_____ 1. I love how in groups, we get bigger than the sum of our parts.

_____ 2. When I have a problem, I like to get a few friends' input on it.

_____ 3. Social causes or national politics matter to me.

_____ 4. On a date, I like to see my partner in a room of people to imagine what comes later.

_____ 5. I can worry if everyone in the group is happy instead of taking care of my needs.

_____ 6. After time alone, I need to get out and share my energy in a group.

_____ 7. When I walk into a room, I can tell who's got the power and who feels left out.

_____ 8. If I'm the one feeling left out, I generally try to work my way in.

_____ 9. If someone disturbs the order of my group, there's going to be a problem.

_____10. I can get reactive around the drab-boring or the overly intense type.

Working with the Instincts

Since the Instincts are more fundamentally important to our motivations and behavior, why not work with them before talking about personality Types? Part of the reason why a study of the Enneagram often starts with the personality Type is that people are eager to dive into understanding this unique system. The Enneagram, with its mystical figure, is captivating. The Arrows for personal development set it apart from mere descriptive typographies. Understanding the Enneagram personality Types provides a tailored roadmap for spiritual growth that people are eager to explore.

Another reason is that the Instincts are really hard to change since they seem so vital to us. "What do you mean all people don't react as I do?" Well, we know they don't, and we step on each others' toes when we don't remember that. Whereas the Passions from personality Type are fueled by Feelings and need to be cajoled at first, the Instincts come from our animalistic Body-based center. These primitive urges don't need gentle coaxing; they need firm resistance. The Instincts are like wild animals with their backs to the wall—they will come out fighting if they feel danger. It is up to our higher mental and feeling centers to firmly tell the Instincts to step down when we are not in real danger. As we found out when we could finally resist these Body urges and stay abstinent, Instincts are like bullies that back down when our Thoughts and Feelings are in alignment.

The way to bring the Instincts into balance so that we can live harmoniously with ourselves and others is to redistribute the energy. The goal is to take a portion of our investment away from our Dominant Instinct and give it to our Repressed one. Here are some tips and tools to decrease your Dominant Instinct and to exercise your Repressed Instinct more.

If Your Dominant Instinct Is	
SP	Don't protect your time and energy as much; disclose yourself more.
SX	Let others have the right of way sometimes; be mindful if you're intruding on others.
SO	Take care of your own needs first; check in with your body on what's good for you; you don't need to lead every group you're part of.
If Your Repressed Instinct Is	
SP	Watch out for HALT (getting too Hungry, Angry, Lonely or Tired) and risk-taking behavior; use more routines to feel organized.
SX	Express yourself more boldly; try more spontaneity; go after what you want.
SO	Watch for skepticism against social action; practice engaging in and trusting some groups.

Instincts x Passions Alchemy

The Enneagram is best studied at the Subtype level to understand the personality because the way that Instincts and Passions combine has such a marked effect on each other. For example, not all Type 4s look alike. While they share Envy as a Passion and can compare themselves to others to determine their worth, the Type 4 with a dominant Sexual Instinct (SX4) will generally judge him- or herself better-than while the Social-driven person (SO4) will usually judge him- or herself less-than. That is because the Sexual Instinct supplies an acquiring/fending off others' energy while the Social Instinct goes toward connection. So SX4 Subtypes will look over their shoulders in a group situation to see who their potential competitors are. The SO4s will do what they can to preserve group harmony—even to the detriment of their own self-esteem. We will examine the 27 Subtypes arising from the combination of the 9 Passions x 3 Instincts in the next chapter.

??? Questions

1. What is your Instinctual Sequence?

2. How comfortable are you operating from your Repressed Instinct? Can you affirm the benefits you'd get if you developed it?

3. Keep daily notes of using your Dominant Instinct less and your Repressed Instinct more using the tips from **Working with the Instincts.** Did you feel more vulnerable not reaching for your Dominant one? How did you tell your Dominant Instinct it was okay to stand down? Record how it feels to *choose* to react differently.

CHAPTER 5

SUBTYPES: Integrating Body and Heart

STEP 5
***Admitted to God, to ourselves, and to
another human being the exact nature of our wrongs.***

All of [X]A.'s Twelve Steps ask us to go contrary to our natural desires . . . they all deflate our egos. When it comes to ego deflation, few Steps are harder to take than Five.[1]

—*Twelve Steps and Twelve Traditions*

When the passion and the dominant instinctual drive come together, they create an even more specific focus of attention, reflecting a particular insatiable need that drives behavior. These subtypes thus reflect three different "subsets" of the patterns of the nine types that provide even more specificity in describing the human personality.[2]

—Beatrice Chestnut, *The Complete Enneagram*

Subtypes

The concept of personality Subtype was introduced in the last chapter. Recall:

Passion of the Type x Dominant Instinct = Subtype
(Feeling-based)   (Body-based)
9 Types' Passion x   3 Instincts   = 27 Subtypes

Why subdivide the nine personality Ego Types further into 27 Subtypes? We first need an accurate self-appraisal to optimally deconstruct what hasn't worked and rebuild a better foundation for living. Some of the main reasons to study our personalities at the Subtype level are that some are so distinct that you may not identify with your Type and give up on the Enneagram as a map for spiritual growth, and very importantly—there are different paths of growth per Subtype. A Type 9 person with Social Instinct Dominant (SO9) will have a different best direction for future growth than a Self-Preservation Instinct Dominant Type 9 (SP9), for example. Meaningful Enneagram work entails getting down to the Subtype level of motivations and behaviors to provide accurate direction.

The Enneagram defines the alchemical combination of Passion x Instinct as Subtype. It is Subtype that largely accounts for variability seen amongst people of the same Type. The reaction between Passion of the Type and Instincts is more than additive. For this reason, teacher Uranio Paes from the Chestnut-Paes Enneagram Academy insists that a multiplication sign be used, and I adopt that convention. The Body-based Instincts collide with the feeling-based Passion of the Type for some interesting reactions.

Some combinations of Instincts and Passion are congruent and amplify each other. For example, the approaching others Sexual Instinct would combine with the assertive Lusty nature of Type 8 to create a real powerhouse. Or the withdrawing energy from the Self Preservation Instinct would combine with the observing Avarice nature of

Type 5 for a quiet bookworm. In Enneagram language, we would refer to the above people as SX8 for a Sexual-Instinct Dominant Type 8 person and SP5 for Self-Preservation Dominant Instinct Type 5. But it is as essential to know the whole Instinctual Sequence because the Repressed Instinct indicates as much of what the person *doesn't* want to deal with as the Dominant Instinct shows what the person demands.

Countertypes

But what happens when the Passion runs contrary to the Instinct? The Subtypes were discovered and elaborated initially to explain the variability seen within Type 6. The Passion of Type 6 is Fear. Fear is one of the most powerful emotions and is referred to in the Big Book as an "evil and corroding thread; the fabric of our existence was shot through with it."[3] If you imagine the powerful Passion of Fear colliding with the Instincts of the "Loyalist" Type 6, there can be huge reactions. Let's look at the combinations:

- SP6- Withdrawing energy from SP x Fearful "Loyalist" = Team-player
- SO6- Connecting energy from SO x Fearful "Loyalist" = Supports *trusted* authority
- SX6- Acquiring energy from SX x Fearful "Loyalist" = Rebels against authority

The grabbing and taking energy coming from the Sexual Instinct runs counter to the Fear in the "Loyalist," and the SX6 is referred to as the Countertype. Eventually, all of the Types' Passions were found to have one Instinct that ran contrary, and all Types have a Countertype. Not all Types have as dramatic a departure from Type behavior as the SX6, who hardly admits Fear at all, but helps explain why a subset of people shows little in common from others in their same Type.

Understanding Countertype is critical to finding traction for spiritual growth using the Enneagram. If you have doubt about your Dominant Instinct from taking a quiz, pay attention to how the Instinct combines with your particular Type's Passion. You will identify your Instinct best by comparing with people sharing your Subtype. When in doubt, work backward by finding yourself in the Subtype descriptions, and then you will know your Dominant Instinct—especially true if you are a Type 4 or 6.

Subtype Summary

Because there is so much valuable information written about the combination of the Type's Passion and Instinct, I recommend one of the excellent resources such as *The Complete Enneagram* by Beatrice Chestnut for full elaboration. She studied under Claudio Naranjo, who was seminal in teaching the modern Enneagram and its Subtypes. Offered here is a brief summary of the 27 Subtypes adapted from Chestnut's book, along with important practices to enlarge your life.

*Countertype: Instinct goes against the Passion of the Type— so they behave differently than others of their Type but are still motivated by their Type's Passion and Virtue.
Instincts: SP=Self-Preservation (Withdrawing)
        SO=Social (Connecting)
        SX=Sexual/One-to-One (Approaching/Fending off)

~~~~~~

TYPE 1: Anger → Serenity

Type 1 General Work: Anger is a primary emotion, and there's nothing wrong with that quick burst. Pay attention to when you feel resentful, though—you're not taking care of your deeper need to be loved despite your human flaws. Adopt some lightness of being from Type 7 and trust that your HP has the perfect plan.

Self-Preservation Type 1 (SP1) "Worry"
High-side: They are responsible, principled and work hard to be beyond reproach. They are perfectionists with high moral standards. They value competence and efficiency and look traditional and neat. They work hard in teams and generally have a plan of the most efficient way to get things done. They are more critical of self, less critical of others and are the warmest Type 1s. What they offer the world is modeling their strong sense of self.

Low-side: They have more anxiety, hence the name "Worry." They plan for worse outcomes, so they can look like Type 6s, except the anxiety is fueled from their Passion of repressed Anger rather than Fear, which fuels Type 6s. Events in their past made SP1s adopt rule books to make them feel safe, and they can feel great resentment when others don't abide by the same rules. The hard-working team member above can get righteous if others in the team aren't pulling their weight or are gaining recognition from political maneuvering. The stress from trying to be perfect may come out in the body as various strains and illnesses.

SP1 Work: Relax your need to control yourself and others so much; be messy sometimes. Try to lay down some of your duties and responsibilities—they're too much for one person. In the Aesop's fable about the dutiful ant judging the irresponsible grasshopper, practice being the grasshopper once in a while.

Social Type 1 (SO1) "Non-Adaptability"
High-side: Instead of instructing others how to be, they attempt to teach correct behavior by modeling it themselves. They are usually traditional and uphold the time-honored way of doing things. They make good teachers because they really apply themselves to their field of study and can inspire others with their own "walking-the-walk." Because SO1s are holding back expressing anger, they appear cooler than the SP1s. Their gift to the world is their strong sense of integrity and real work ethic, often for social causes.

Low-side: Their "Non-Adaptability" nickname comes from their rigid idea of what is right (they are!) and what is wrong. Even though their Dominant Instinct is Social, SO1s hold themselves apart from the group and find it hard to be in the middle. It's as if their Anger has one foot on the accelerator, but their social need to be seen as "good" keeps one foot on the brake. SO1s tend to be intellectual, like Type 5s, but their competence is fueled by exasperation that others don't make the effort to master their field as much as they do.

SO1 Work: In groups, sit back occasionally and see what happens when the group does things another way—you don't always have to be the leader or the teacher. In one-to-one conversations, use your curiosity to find out what the other knows. On your next walk, refuse to stare at or pick up any trash (or dirty dishes in the sink at home)—let it be all right that others are slobs sometimes.

*Sexual/One-to-One Type 1 (SX1) "Zeal"

High-side: This Subtype is in touch with their anger, so they seem big and powerful. The reason that they are the Countertype within Type 1 is that they don't have one foot on the brake of their Anger. They are strong, full of vitality and are action-oriented. They can use their magnetism to rally a group to a cause because they wholeheartedly believe in it. SX1s are so sure of their cause that others often follow them. Like most One-to-One Instinctual Types, their energy burns hot and intense. At their best, they use their energy for sweeping societal reforms.

Low-side: The other name besides "Zeal" is "Reformer" because this kind of perfectionist "takes great pains . . . and gives them to another." They are plagued doubly by seeing what's wrong in the world and trying the impossible task of making others do something about it. They can justify their Anger and attempt to control others by being on the moral high ground. Prior to getting into recovery, this Subtype could lead a double life, completely out of sync with the high morals claimed by day.

SX1 Work: Before throwing yourself into some cause, check that you're not trying to avoid looking at something within. Once you get rolling, periodically check in with your Head and your emotions to make sure you're not steamrolling yourself or others. You were given a gift of lots of vitality, so use it *for* people, not *against* them, by telling them how to live.

~~~~~~

TYPE 2: Pride → Humility

Type 2 General Work: It's humble to know that you can and should take care of your own needs. What you give to others is what you deserve, so use some of Type 4's authenticity to advocate for yourself. When you feel hurt or resentful, it's the sign that you've been giving with expectations, and it's time to tap into your HP's fuller love.

*Self-Preservation Type 2 (SP2) "Privilege"

High-side: This Countertype doesn't look like other Type 2s who show their desire to make others like them. The withdrawing energy from the Self-Preservation Instinct counters the usual seeking of attention to bolster Pride. They are charming and are disarming in their innocence. Their gift to others is their openness, which in turn encourages openness in others.

Low-side: Their seeming openness actually has elements of fear. On one hand, they feel "Privileged," and their Pride assumes that others want to give. But on the other hand, they are ambivalent about both giving and receiving help. They sense they have sold some of their freedom to be loved and then crave that freedom back. They can play "helpless" to get others to care for them and be deeply hurt when others fail to meet their needs.

SP2 Work: Consciously take care of your own needs, learn to set boundaries. Check in with yourself whether people deserve your trust, and if they do, try not to withdraw if they disappoint you but directly communicate your needs to them.

Social Type 2 (SO2) "Ambition"

High-side: This Type is not passive but actively pursues success. They are often intellectual, influential leaders. They naturally exude Pride and can look like Types 3 or 8 in being successful, only with more demonstrations of vulnerability. They are good at social networking. Their gift is harnessing their helping desires for the larger social good.

Low-side: Their "Ambition" to be leaders betrays an underlying need for approval. By becoming indispensable to so many, they earn adulation, which feeds their Pride. They can get carried away with their own power and step on the toes of others. SO2s can lose touch with their feelings in workaholism and can "give to get."

SO2 Work: Recognize when work and giving are distractions from deeper needs and vulnerability—you don't present as vulnerable. Get in touch with your softer side and needs. You don't need to buy love with anything.

Sexual/One-to-One Type 2 (SX2) "Aggressive-Seductive"

High-side: The outer-directed energy from Type 2 combines with the acquiring energy from the Instinct to make for real charmers. These gregarious people are sure of their magnetism and use it overtly. The recipients of this great energy feel special and singled out. Their gift is bringing intensity and aliveness to any interaction.

Low-side: Although they delight in being "Aggressive-Seductive" and attractive, part of them knows that they are driven by Pride to conquer—even those they aren't that interested in. This being "on" so much of the time can cause depression when their energy runs low. Many people don't mind being caught up in the SX2's sex kitten or tomcat wiles, but in the end, it hurts the SX2s themselves by objectifying and being objectified.

SX2 Work: Check your motives in a relationship—are you truly interested in the other or just as a mirror to reflect back adulation and how they make you feel about yourself? Invest some of your energy in activities with friends or something which feeds your soul. Downplay your appearance sometimes. Let your friends know when you're having a down day.

~~~~~~

TYPE 3: Self-Deceit → Veracity

Type 3 General Work: Veracity means telling yourself the truth about who you are and what you value. As a Type 3 put it, it's Fake → Real. Type 3s have been on a treadmill of their own making for so long—they're afraid to slow down. Self-Deceit about their inflated place in the universe is likely covering fears of inadequacy. If Type 3s are brave, they can turn around to address Fear and find their Type 6 Courage to discover that they really are stand-out people.

*Self-Preservation Type 3 (SP3) "Security"

High-side: They work hard to earn the material things that mean "Security" to them. They are the Countertype because the self-promoting energy from their Type's Passion contradicts the withdrawing energy from the Instinct, leaving SP3s wanting recognition but also to appear modest. They are over-achievers to prove to themselves that they deserve their high reputation. Their gift is the class and quality that they bring to their endeavors.

Low-side: In their rush to succeed, they can be very impatient and shut down to their own feelings. Self-Deceit is not acknowledging how much they do for show while appearing self-effacing. Their rigid thinking and ultra-responsibility can make them look like Type 1s, but they conform to an external set of rules rather than Type 1's internal moral compass.

SP3 Work: Slow down to let the fear surface—you can deal with it, and once you do, you'll free up that anxious energy. Learn to delegate at work and ask for help at home. Take periodic retreat weekends to get in touch with what *you* want for your own life. SP3s have reinvented themselves by starting new careers based on their values instead of inherited ones.

Social Type 3 (SO3) "Prestige"

High-side: These Type 3s stand out in their work and social circles. They are well-spoken and put together. Their people skills often promote them to being leaders. They work hard and are more overt than SP3s in seeking recognition. Their gift is their grace under pressure, even if it takes a personal toll, and the vitality they bring to their groups.

Low-side: Their crafting an image of "Prestige" can be at the expense of their own spiritual development. Their natural leader abilities mean they usually want to be at the top and get impatient with others who lack their vision. They lose track of their own feelings in trying to look so put together and by collecting people for Prestige rather than deeper values.

SO3 Work: Focus more on "be a human *be*-ing, not a human *do*-ing." Practice showing your flaws to people you trust and then people at work. You don't need to take charge of every group you belong to. If you can extend compassion and patience to your own inner critic, you can also grant it to others.

Sexual/One-to-One Type 3 (SX3) "Charisma"

High-side: These Type 3s are more willing to put their own success behind the ones they support. They are appealing, like the SX2s, in a more classical style. Their name "Charisma" is from the Greek for "divine gift, grace and beauty"—and their name says it all.

Low-side: They spend much of their energy pleasing others and can also suffer emotional burnout like SP3s. SX3s are even more emotional and yet more afraid of their feelings. Packaging themselves for others can lead to real self-alienation and the sense they don't know who they are.

SX3 Work: You must find a way to shift from looking at yourself as if others were seeing you to how *you* see you. As for all Type 3s, if you have Courage to face your fear of earning love, you can connect with your feelings and come to know your own meaning in life.

~~~~~~

TYPE 4: Envy → Equanimity

Type 4 General Work: Type 4s are so emotionally attuned to others; they intensely crave to be seen by others in return. To give them firm boundaries of what is theirs and what is another's, they need to draw from the strength and conviction from Type 1 for Serenity. Subtypes of Type 4 are very distinct from each other.

*Self-Preservation Type 4 (SP4) "Tenacity"

High-side: The Countertype SP4s are less conscious of Envy because they work hard to get what they lack. They are less dramatic than other Type 4s and are even called the "sunny 4s" for their "Tenacity" in the face of adversity. Their gift is their great ability to go deep and model feelings for others.

Low-side: They gain identity for taking on the emotional load of others in the family and then in the world. Another name for this Subtype is "Dauntless" because they throw themselves into risky behavior and glamorize the dark side. It's as if no one came and recognized that they were suffering as children, so now they've upped the stakes.

SP4 Work: Although you didn't get crucial recognition growing up, it's time to give yourself the tenderness and compassion to stop hiding behind a mask. It's all right to let others know when you feel vulnerable and in need of help.

Social Type 4 (SO4) "Inadequacy"
High-side: They feel things deeply and more openly show Envy and suffering. SO4s are dramatic and have a flair for artistic and emotional expression—so much so that they can put other's inarticulate feelings into words. They offer their rich and multi-layered emotional life as their gift to the world.

Low-side: In the comparison game of Envy, they often see their "Inadequacy." This can be frustrating and mystifying to loved ones because SO4s really are unique people. SO4s have a push-pull conflict—they would like to join in but see themselves with "that mysterious barrier we could neither surmount nor understand."[4] They idealize what they don't have but hold themselves apart. Embracing suffering is an attempt to feel connected with themselves, but further isolates them from others.

SO4 Work: Having tenacity when one is in the middle of unavoidable pain is strength. But as it says in the Big Book, "avoid then, the deliberate manufacture of misery."[5] When sadness comes on, make gratitude lists of what's in front of you right now. You can handle deep emotions, so work on anger and joy to balance fear and sadness.

Sexual/One-to-One Type 4 (SX4) "Competition"
High-side: The One-to-One Instinct lets this Type go after what they want rather than waiting on others. They are assertive and use Envy as a motivator for "Competition." Their gift is their direct and honest approach to life.

Low-side: When they compare in Envy, they generally take the superior position. They can be reactive, and if hurt, they're going to complain about it. Instead of sadness, their top emotion is anger.

SX4 Work: Get in touch with the vulnerability underneath your superior attitude. The solidness offered by Type 1 can balance the reactivity of your strong emotions and bring you calmness from your Virtue of Equanimity.

~~~~~~

TYPE 5: Greed-Avarice → Nonattachment

Type 5 General Work: They see the world as depleting, which makes it so. Type 5s won't give to others until they feel that they have enough themselves, so they need the Innocence from Type 8 to open up.

Self-Preservation Type 5 (SP5) "Castle"

High-side: These usually introverted Types can be warm and funny when they're secure. They are intelligent and well-spoken—if a little reserved. Their gift to the world is their depth of thought before stating an opinion and simplifying complex ideas.

Low-side: They are hyper-conscious of how much energy they have left and can withdraw abruptly into their "Castle," causing confusion to loved ones. They are private, and their Greed and Avarice closes them to both giving and receiving. They try not to ask for much and get aggressive when they think people ask too much of them.

SP5 Work: Relax boundaries and try to be more open. Get in touch with your fear that you don't have enough time and energy and how that becomes a self-fulfilling prophecy. Practice giving before receiving—not with favors but at the emotional level.

Social Type 5 (SO5) "Totem"

High-side: They are more comfortable in groups than the SP5s, but their primary focus is more on the subject material than people in the group. They are brilliant at understanding systems of knowledge, and their gift to the world is conveying them to others.

Low-side: As with all of the Types in the Head triad, SO5s hold anxiety. "Totem" means creating a body of knowledge that they Greedily hold onto to ward off the feared meaninglessness of life.

SO5 Work: Accept the idea that factoids can't keep us safe. Tap into your Holy Omniscience that while our intellectual pursuits are important, they're minuscule in the scale of all there is to know. Your intellectualism can be blocking you from forming "a true partnership with another human being."[6]

*Sexual/One-to-One Type 5 (SX5) "Confidence"
High-side: The One-to-One Instinct provides a lot of vitality and a need for intense relationships. SX5s are more vibrant and expressive, often in an emotional or artistic way. Their gift is a positive blend of a keen intellect coupled with passionate zest.

Low-side: The withdrawing tactic from Greed fights the Instinct's approaching energy— resulting in the Countertype. These Type 5s look more like Type 4s with their vibrancy and emotionalism. Greed makes them want to test the loyalty of their partners. "Confidence" means trusting the other with secrets but then testing if the partner will stay close. For example, SX5s could go away, hoping their partner will come after them or do something destructive in the relationship to see if the other will still love them.

SX5 Work: Allow yourself to feel the fear in relationships and open up anyway. It's hard for you to trust in a relationship, and you'll need to borrow from Type 8's Virtue of Innocence to make the leap of faith. Check yourself when you set up traps to test your loved ones.

~~~~~~

TYPE 6: Fear → Courage
Type 6 General Work: As was said for Anger, Fear is a primary emotion, and there are times when it's necessary. But as Mark Twain put it, "I've had a lot of worries in my life, most of which never happened." So it's the False Evidence Appearing Real obsession that needs to be overcome with Courage. The Right Action Virtue from Type 9 can break the obsessive worrying by getting grounded in the Body to walk through Fear. Subtypes of Type 6 are very distinct from each other.

Self-Preservation Type 6 (SP6) "Warmth"

High-side: Their name "Warmth" comes from the fact that these Type 6s are warm and avoid confrontations in a group. They build alliances for protection. Their gift to the world is their projection of peace, calmness and unity.

Low-side: These are the most fearful of the Type 6s— their outer calmness hides an inner torment of fear, doubt and flares of anger. They are hesitant to make decisions on their own. If you ask them a question, they'll ask a question to clarify. They say that they're careful who they let into their inner circle because then they'd have to worry about them.

SP6 Work: Rely more on your own decisions and strength. The problem with the strategy of forecasting doom to be safe is that it robs you of the ability to act and *be* safe: "Thinking the World is Dangerous Makes It So." Work on the suggestions for catastophizing in Chapter 6.

Social Type 6 (SO6) "Duty"

High-side: They are supportive of authority when trusted as competent. They are intellectual and principled and are efficient in a crisis. Their gift is to have a calming effect on others in the group by demonstrating assurance.

Low-side: Their name "Duty" comes from relying on a code of behavior or ideology to overcome doubt. Instead of being indecisive like SP6s, they can have their minds too made up. They can cope with Fear with intolerance and rigidity and therefore look like Type 1s—but where Type 1s have an internal sense of right and wrong, SO6s will cite the rules.

SO6 Work: Choose pleasure over duty more; act more from your gut rather than your Head. As it says in the Big Book, "[W]e find that our thinking will, as time passes, be more and more on the plane of inspiration. We come to rely upon it."[7]

*Sexual/One-to-One Type 6 (SX6) "Strength/Beauty"
High-side: Usually, they are self-confident with the intense spark from their Instinct. They devote time and energy to their "Strength or Beauty" to feel secure. Being "good" is defined according to their own rules. Their gift is being skillful and ready for any emergency.

Low-side: This Countertype covers fear by being intimidating and choosing risky situations. They can look powerful like Type 8s, but underneath, they are motivated by fear. "The best defense is a good offense" could have meant throwing the first punch back in the day. They trust themselves over others and rebel against authority.

SX6 Work: Get more comfortable with letting down your guard. See if you can trace times when you're angry back to Fear. Try the suggestions for anger-related fixations in Chapter 6.

~~~~~~

TYPE 7: Gluttony → Sobriety
Type 7 General Work: Gluttony is the *dis-ease*, the restlessness and anxiety of looking for the next thing to make you happy. You benefit from adding Type 5's gravitas for moderation in your thoughts and emotions—which is Sobriety.

Self-Preservation Type 7 (SP7) "Keepers of the Castle"
High-side: They are cheerful, fun-loving, pragmatic and good at networking to get what they want. They have an earthy and sensuous presence. Back in the day, they were experts at enjoying the "high" side of life (pun intended). Their gift to the world is their upbeat energy and "can-do" spirit.

Low-side: They can be shocked to hear that their friends see them as self-consumed, usually doing what the SP7 wants in the relationship. Since they want what they want *now*, they can go *around* authority instead of against it. During low energy times, they can isolate as "Keepers of the Castle" and become fairly cynical.

SP7 Work: Ask directly for what you want instead of trying to manipulate for it. The rules *do* apply to you, so try some acceptance of them. In the Aesop's fable about the dutiful ant and the irresponsible grasshopper, practice being the ant more often. Although you come across as emotional, you can be shut down to your negative emotions, so spend quiet time getting to know them.

*Social Type 7 (SO7) "Sacrifice"

High-side: They are visionary idealists who "Sacrifice" their Gluttony for others and seem more grounded than other Type 7s. This Countertype doesn't seem hedonistic like the SP7s but rather like the Type 2 Helper. They eagerly participate in altruistic groups, and their gift is lending their enthusiasm and vision to these groups.

Low-side: Fear and anxiety are underneath all of the Types in the Head triad. So while SO7s look self-sacrificing, they are also conscious of selfishness and the need for applause. They can be the outlier in the groups they join and move on when the novelty has worn off.

SO7 Work: Check your motive under self-sacrifice, and how getting involved with external things can be a distraction from interior work. Use meditation to really face your FEAR and anxiety.

Sexual/One-to-One Type 7 (SX7) "Suggestibility"

High-side: They are optimistic and very idealistic. Whereas the SP7s are earthy, the SX7s have their "head in the clouds." They strive for a mystical union in their intimate relationships. Their gift is bringing enthusiasm and the belief that the glass is more than half full to the world.

Low-side: Another name for "Suggestibility" is being gullible. SX7s have such a need to see only the bright side that they can be taken advantage of. They also have unaddressed FEAR and can be restless and easily bored. Instead of savoring what they have, they may feel that they're missing out on something even better.

SX7 Work: Observe when you're living in a fantasy or using your intellect to rationalize. Bring your attention back to the here and now. Make friends with the mundane. When fear, sadness or anger comes up, use your curiosity to examine why.

~~~~~~

TYPE 8: Lust → Innocence

Type 8 General Work: Types 8s have spent a lifetime exerting power over their environment. Instead of the repressed Anger of Type 1, their Anger is direct—Lust is Ego going after what it wants. They need to use Type 2's Humility to return to Innocence—starting each day fresh and each encounter with a clean slate.

Self-Preservation Type 8 (SP8) "Satisfaction"

High-side: They do what it takes to satisfy their needs for the physical and financial necessities of life. They are self-sufficient and possess a quiet strength, not displaying a lot of emotion. Their gift is their strength, enveloping loved ones in their force field.

Low-side: They feel the urgency for "Satisfaction" of their needs and can be steamrollers if others frustrate them. When off-center, they retaliate against perceived harms.

SP8 Work: When we got into recovery, we had to face that our Egos alone were insufficient to save us and that asking for help was the strongest thing to do. To make spiritual progress, you'll need the same reframing. Work at expressing vulnerability more and get in touch with your softer side—you've already proven that you are strong.

*Social Type 8 (SO8) "Solidarity"

High-side: This Countertype diverts the Lust and anger shown by the other Subtypes into helping others. They are warm and friendly and can look like helpers until someone under their care is threatened. Their gift is being sociable leaders that others trust to have their backs.

Low-side: They go against the dominant patriarchal power and can be quite aggressive when protecting the underdog. The way that Type 6s worry about the people in their group, Type 8s feel that they have to protect them—they demand "Solidarity" and loyalty in their group. They show their care better in groups than in one-to-one relationships because they are afraid of their own vulnerability in closer relationships.

SO8 Work: Work as hard to take care of your own needs as you do for others. Be careful of your desire to control others and over manage people in your group. Types 8s are so confidant in their Instinctual bodies that they assume they're right—they need to stop and question their thoughts and feelings to get the bigger picture.

Sexual/One-to-One Type 8 (SX8) "Possession"

High-side: They make charismatic leaders and are passionate and emotional. They don't mind being seen as the "bad boys" as they are unconventional and have a strong presence. Their gift is exuding such an aura of power that others want to follow.

Low-side: The SX8 is one of the most intense Types. "Possession" happens in friends and intimate relationships as they are prone to jealousy. In an argument, they can't leave well enough alone but push to reach a solution—their solution.

SX 8 Work: Watch your desire to be a contrarian and act before thinking. You'll need Humility from Type 2 and the pause before acting from Type 5 for balance. When you're trying to control "people, places and things," slow down to connect with your possible hurt feelings.

~~~~~~

TYPE 9: Sloth → Right Action
Type 9 General Work: As with the other Types in the central position of their center of intelligence (Types 3, 6, and 9), Type 9s need to get more in touch with their own center. They have gone to sleep to their own Instinctual power, their own anger and their own gut reactions. They need to reach for Type 3s self-honesty to advocate for their own needs.

Self-Preservation Type 9 (SP9) "Appetite"
High-side: They are warm and funny and recharge with time spent alone. They are practical, down to earth and try not to make big deals of anything. Their gift is adding harmony to groups and relationships that they're in and are often the shoulder others cry on.

Low-side: They use their "Appetite" of food, naps and zoning out routines to substitute for the love they feel they didn't get. They have stronger personalities than the other Type 9s and keep their power by being stubborn.

SP9 Work: Check in with yourself at set times throughout the day: what are you thinking, feeling and how's your body right now? If you can't tell what your next Right Action is, fake it til you make it by doing the first thing that seems indicated.

*Social Type 9 (SO9) "Participation"
High-side: They are sociable and encourage "Participation" by their own hard work—and downplay that they're working so hard. They are good in business meetings by mediating and making sure that the minority opinion gets heard. Their gift is bringing cohesiveness and harmony to their groups.

Low-side: They often hide their own needs to please the group; they "go along to get along." When they take their peacemaking too far, they can be wishy-washy. SO9s can use workaholism to avoid problems at home—and, more importantly, their own feelings of sadness.

SO9 Work: Meet your own needs before non-essential sidetracks. Start the day with the three things you most want to get done and <u>do</u> them. If you're overworking, check in with yourself with your thoughts, your body and especially with your fear of not belonging.

Sexual/One-to-One Type 9 (SX9) "Fusion"
High-side: They are introverted, gentle souls who show their emotions readily. They get their name "Fusion" from the intense concentration they bring to intimate relationships. Their gift is being able to form a special bond with one person.

Low-side: "Fusion" is merging by adopting the likes and attitudes of the other instead of your own values. It is counterproductive to your aim of a vibrant and authentic relationship because there is not enough of *you* there.

SX9 Work: Take time apart to reaffirm your own needs. Step into your power instead of acting on the sly. By being more substantial in all relationships—at work or home, you give the other person or group something to push back against for more satisfying relationships. Get in touch with your fear of separation, possibly the separation anxiety that started in childhood.

~~~~~~

By understanding the complex interaction between Body-based Instinct and Feeling-based Passion, we can work at the Subtype level to really root out old patterns and find our best path for growth. As was noted in the last chapter, whether we're working on the Virtues from our home Type, Back-Arrow, Wings or Forward-Arrow Type, we generally keep our same Instinctual Sequence. So look at the suggestions to try for your own Subtype and your Back-Arrow Subtype for your personalized path. For example, if you're a SP7 you would recognize when fear led you to get your needs met covertly from your own Subtype AND practice lowering of your boundaries and showing your needs from your SP5 Back-Arrow Subtype.

Subtypes show strategies from the Body and Heart centers. We can begin to discern from which center our over-reacting is coming. If your behavior doesn't make sense coming from your Feeling-centered Type, consider if it's coming from your Instinct—and therefore needs a firm approach. Working at the Subtype level helps to balance the Body and Heart. Integrity comes from having more of our centers in harmony with each other internally. And externally, integrity comes when our insides match how we behave in the world.

Building Community

The Enneagram does not have a confession of past wrongs component. We *can* avail ourselves of an Enneagram coach or therapist, attend Enneagram workshops or start our own informal group of friends in recovery exploring how to improve our conscious contact with our HPs using the Enneagram. The reason that such support is helpful is the same as in our program of recovery. Without frequent reminders of our spiritual goal, we might give up or backslide into former easier behavior. As in our recovery meetings, we share hope with others on good days and borrow hope that we are indeed making progress on our bad days. Another reason for practicing the Enneagram work in a group is similar to what the *Twelve Steps and Twelve Traditions* says in Step 5: we might be practicing rationalization if we're working alone.[8] Participating in an Enneagram group can help solidify our spiritual goal and provides a practice area to try out new behavior. Oh, and it's fun!

??? Questions

1. How has knowing your Subtype clarified what to do next beyond the recommendations for just your Type?

2. Try practicing the new behaviors recommended both for your Subtype and your Back-Arrow Subtype in the **Subtype Summary** and make notes on your progress. What did you discover?

3. Knowing that your Feeling-based Passions need gentler redirection and the Body-based Instincts require firmness—can you sense whether your behavior is coming from the Feelings or Body center and modify your behavior appropriately?

CHAPTER 6

MENTAL FIXATIONS: Obsession of the Mind

STEP 6
*Were entirely ready to have God remove
all these defects of character.*

Therefore, the main problem of the alcoholic
centers in his mind, rather than in his body.[1]

—*Alcoholics Anonymous*

We lose touch with seeing the objective reality ... We end up
developing instead, a lower mental pattern, called fixation ...
What is fixation? It's basically a filter that limits me seeing
things from another angle.[2]

—Uranio Paes, "Understanding
the Enneagram Fixations"

The Mental Center

So far we've gone over how our Body-based Instincts and Feeling-based Passions can trip us up. Our Instincts are so instantaneous that they may not phrase their demands in words. Remember when the obsession to use or act codependently was upon you. For a long time, we had no mental defense. It was just a tidal wave of Body-based energy landing us in the same old spot. We learned in Chapter 4 that we deal with Instincts firmly, letting them know our higher centers are in charge. Then in Chapters 1, 2 and 3, we studied the Heart-based Passions. These Passions definitely have a voice—anything from Type 1's "Did you see what he just pulled?!" to Type 3's "Do know who I am?!" Our Ego may only voice this internally, but it's loud and clear. We learned to redirect our Feelings slowly at first, practicing the Virtues more over time.

The Head-based Ego also has a voice, but it is more subtle and rational sounding. In our using days, this rational voice stepped in to bolster what our Instincts and Feelings had already decided to do. The mental center probably put up some resistance, like "Don't do this, you know how you'll feel in the morning . . ." But when it knew it had lost, said, "You already started today. We can start fresh tomorrow." Nowadays, we are trying to get over our addiction to Ego. The mental resistance to this task is just as sly and subtle. Our Ego wants to stay in charge, to maintain the status quo and will enlist all three centers of Body, Heart and Head to do so.

The Instincts show the first differentiation from Essence, and are our Body's fight to survive. Passions represent our second layer of armor, bringing us farther from Essence, and are the Heart center's cry to have our needs met. The Fixations are the final coping strategy from our Head center and strategize and rationalize *how* to get our needs met.

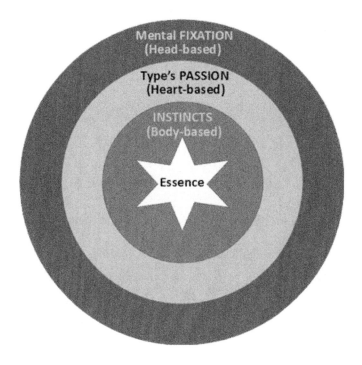

The Fixations

The mental Fixations per Type sound similar to the emotional Passions because they are strategies to protect us from the suffering of our Passion. But since they employ a different way to keep the Ego in charge, the Fixations require a different strategy to outsmart. We will learn one possible strategy soon, but let's put the Fixations into everyday language before we look at the Enneagram terminology. The Fixations, like the Passions, reflect a lack of Faith that our HP or the Universe is really taking care of things, much less our little selves. Our internal voice from our mental Fixation might sound like:

Type	The Voice of your Fixation
1	If I'm not on top of things, they will never get done right.
2	If I keep taking care of you, eventually you'll see what I need and reciprocate.
3	I have arrived—my HP can take the day off.
4	I want to get out of myself but get overwhelmed and trapped inside.
5	I doubt my needs will be met, so I'll figure things out on my own.
6	Arrrrrghhhhhhhhhhhhhh . . . Constant hum of Arrrrrghhhhhhhh.
7	This time my little plans and designs will make me feel at peace.
8	I believe that everyone gets theirs in the end; I'll help in the meantime.
9	What's the point of all this work—I'm not sure it or I matter in the end.

The Enneagram of Holy Ideas

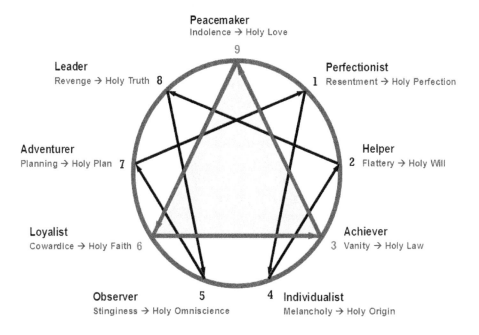

Look at your Holy Idea—does it appeal to you? As we saw that each Type brings a Virtue from the Feeling center, each Type also brings a particular gift from the Thought center. And each Type has a low-functioning side known as the Fixation. The mental Ego Fixation is the specific way we lose sight that we are part of a bigger whole. We find that the Fixation used to cope with the pain of our Passion is *causing* the very thing we seek to avoid! Although we might call our mental fixations our "core beliefs," they are not truly our core since that is pure Essence. Once we uncover these wrong assumptions of reality, we can model for others our Holy Idea or mental connection with our Higher Power.

Pay attention to your home Type and your Back-Arrow Type of Fixation in the following descriptions.

~~~~~~

Fixations to Holy Ideas per Type

TYPE 1: "Perfectionist"   Resentment → Holy Perfection

Fixation: Resentment- Resentment covers the anguish caused by the Passion of Anger. Resentment is giving a socially acceptable justification as to why we are angry. To re- "sentir" means "to feel again," so it's compounding the pain of feeling that something is not right in the world by having to feel it over and over again. We all need real anger to set boundaries. But why would we hold onto anger if not to try to make something right with the power of thinking it so? The obsessive thought is the *illusion of control*: Type 1s are trying to make their world safe by holding onto a rule book—which few others pay attention to. They carry past harms done to them and need a way of releasing that energy to lead unburdened lives. By covering Anger with Resentment, we get stuck in feeling frustrated and create the negativity we're trying to correct.

Holy Idea: Holy Perfection- Everything is all right—perfect—how it is right now. The flow of the universe is right on track, and every person will have what she or he needs. Even the hard times reveal that in every Ego problem is an inherent solution—our HP's.

TYPE 2: "Helper"   Flattery → Holy Will

Fixation: Flattery- Flattery covers the pain from hurt Pride. It's based on the fear that if Type 2s don't smile and give and give, they will not be loved, and their own needs will not be met. The fixation is an obsession with others' feelings—like their survival is based on how they are seen and treated by others instead of firmly rooted in what their HP or they themselves want. It's the compulsive feeling-thought that "I am my brother's keeper." By covering Pride with Flattery, we further alienate those we hope to draw near when they feel manipulated.

Holy Idea: Holy Will- It is not within the power of any of us to *make* someone else happy. Turning over our will to the higher Will means trusting that everyone we care about, and we ourselves will be taken care of with or without our intervention. Type 2s have the gift of mirroring this trust in the bigger picture.

TYPE 3: "Achiever"   Vanity → Holy Law

Fixation: Vanity- Vanity covers the pain of self Deceit like the way we cover our inferiority complex with egomania. The self-esteem that Type 3s seek comes from the mistaken idea that they *must* perform or be discarded. There is an obsession with proving themselves to people they hold in even higher esteem. Vanity is the fear and arrogance that the HP is not moving fast enough, and therefore, Type 3s must make things happen. In using Vanity to cover self Deceit, we end up feeling worse about ourselves because we know we don't deserve the reputation we have crafted to win love.

Holy Idea: Holy Law- There are huge dynamic forces in the universe, and we can hope to be but channels of them. Type 3s can connect with real hope—hope for themselves and their place in the universe that requires no tricks or power plays. Fitting oneself into the Law or flow of the universe relieves Type 3s from their heavy self-imposed burden.

TYPE 4: "Individualist"   Melancholy → Holy Origin

Fixation: Melancholy- Melancholy covers Envy's pain by making what we "can't have" bitter-sweet. Melancholy is a happy-sad emotion and tugs Type 4s in two directions: focusing on what they can never have and glorifying their estrangement. They struggle with the idea that they must be truly special people just to break even. There is an obsession with seeing the self as "outsider." Using Melancholy to cover the Envy of not having a complete self without reference to others ensures that their fear of being estranged comes true.

Holy Idea: Holy Origin- While we have so many superficial differences, we all share the same divine spark. There is a coming home feeling to Holy Origin—we can all partake equally in the banquet of life—we have nothing to prove at this level.

TYPE 5: "Observer"   Stinginess → Holy Omniscience

Fixation: Stinginess- Stinginess, or holding oneself back, covers the pain of Greed and creates a closed system. To not become depleted, Type 5s carefully meter out their time, space and connections with others. The mental fixation has a hoarding quality, which can keep this Type stuck with old ideas and resentments. There is an obsession to not see the self as needy out of fear that one's needs won't be met. Using Stinginess to cover Greed makes the fear of limited resources in the universe come true.

Holy Idea: Holy Omniscience- Knowing everything, being open to everything, letting people, things and ideas come and go—then we no longer live in a hostile universe all alone.

TYPE 6: "Loyalist"   Cowardice → Holy Faith

Fixation: Cowardice- Cowardice covers the pain of Fear by making excuses for why we couldn't face something. It is a shrinking back from life fixation—or for the counterphobic Type 6, it's reactively challenging a situation. There is an obsession that if the Type 6 person plans enough for everything that could go wrong, then that Type can rest. But there are always new Fears on the horizon. We all need to address real fear but worrying ahead of time is False Evidence Appearing Real (FEAR). Using Cowardice to avoid Fear incapacitates us, and then we *are* incapable of acting.

Holy Idea: Holy Faith- We've all heard that courage is not the absence of fear but walking through it. In the rooms, we've heard that Faith is Fear that has said its prayers. The Holy Faith of Type 6 reminds us that "Everything will be alright in the end. If it's not alright, it's not the end."

TYPE 7: "Adventurer"   Planning → Holy Plan

Fixation: Planning- Planning how to satisfy Gluttony is doomed because Gluttony is insatiable. The Type 7's Ego Plans are always around the next corner, always restless and dissatisfied. The fixation is that the individual alone knows what will make her or him happy. This strategy of living in the future may sound like Type 4s, but Type 7 does so with near-manic exuberance instead of melancholy. This self-centered drive to Plan robs us of the ability to savor what is here now.

Holy Idea: Holy Plan- By calming down, enjoying the journey and waiting to see what our HP's Plan for us could be, we can see the beauty along the way. Type 7s can use their innate curiosity to see the everyday miracles here and now.

TYPE 8: "Leader"   Revenge → Holy Truth

Fixation: Revenge- Revenge is an attempt to channel the power of Lust. Type 8s are constantly looking for power inequalities in life. They have a fixed belief that they themselves are the appointed ones to set right an injustice. If Lust is the grabbing and taking nature in us that tries to ensure security, looking for injustice where none was intended starts the fight.

Holy Idea: Holy Truth- Instead of setting up power plays to feel some control in life, Type 8s need balance to "accept the things we cannot change" and remember that there is a divine Truth beyond what they can see.

TYPE 9: "Peacemaker"   Indolence → Holy Love

Fixation: Indolence- Indolence, from the Latin for "freedom from pain," is the mental cover-up for Sloth. Change takes hard work, and Type 9s distract themselves from their own potentially painful work by fixating on others' needs. Rather than the Type 2s pattern of "giving to get," Type 9s go to sleep to their own important contributions toward life. They have a fixed belief that they don't truly matter. Using Indolence supposedly to create harmony creates disharmony from their Slothful lack of participation.

Holy Idea: Holy Love- Stepping aside so that others can receive more divine Love is not honest. We are all equally deserving of Holy Love and each responsible for co-creating life. Type 9s hold a special place at the top of the Enneagram and are needed to step joyfully into the light and claim Holy Love.

~~~~~~

Calming the "Obsession of the Mind"

Working against the Fixation and toward our Holy Idea will require careful attention to that cunning, baffling and powerful voice within. As was said, the Passions are much louder inside. One good way to get in touch with this mental Fixation is to first feel the discomfort or pain in our feeling-center, and then track it back to the wrong thinking that preceded it. We'll check if our emotions are balanced and healthy—appropriate to what's going on—in the next chapter. But if you pause every time you're disturbed, you might see a pattern of thinking that creates the problem. A given situation could leave one person angry and irate and another baffled and hurt. It's the same stimulus, but our minds interpret things differently. That would be fine unless we have patterns, or obsessions of the mind, that cause us reoccurring harm. Uncovering our Essence is like peeling the onion—and a good place to start will be at this outermost armor of our Mental Fixation.

Availing yourself of ways to calm reactive mental patterns is worthwhile, with lasting effects for the rest of your life. There is a whole alphabet soup of techniques that can pinpoint our unnecessary interpretations—our wrong thinking. Other references for helpful techniques are listed in the **Resources** section in the back—including Acceptance and Commitment Therapy (ACT), Dialectical Behavioral Therapy (DBT), Eye Movement Desensitization and Reprocessing (EMDR) and Emotional Freedom Technique (EFT). We'll look at Cognitive Behavioral Therapy (CBT) since it is a powerful method to disentangle our unhealthy fixed ideas that habitually produce the same painful feelings.[3]

Cognitive Behavioral Therapy

CBT was pioneered in the 1960s to help people with various reoccurring painful emotional and behavioral problems, including addiction, stemming from their thinking patterns. CBT has a reputation of assisting primarily thinking Types, perhaps due to having "Cognitive" as part of its name, but it has been misapprehended. Thinking has two main functions: cognition—taking in sensory data from the environment—and *evaluation*. The evaluation function helps make us human by choosing how to respond with both Feelings *and* Thoughts to attain what we value and avoid what we disvalue. So it's not a matter of stomping on our Feelings with our Thoughts—but it's noticing when we confuse the evaluation process with the facts, and see problems that don't exist. CBT starts with **Awareness** of how we choose to (mis)interpret situations and suggests a remedy for these "hot thoughts." I recommend getting *Thoughts & Feelings* by McKay, Davis and Fanning.[4] It offers a straightforward workbook approach with treatment modules specific for anything from anger, anxiety disorders, depression to worry and stress. Following is a summary from their book:

Thought Pattern	Remedy
Filtering	Focus on the good
Polarizing, black & white	Think in percents
Overgeneralizing	No labels; quantify
Mind-reading	Ask, no assumptions without words
Catastrophizing, what if	What are the odds
Magnifying, can't cope	I can handle it with my HP
Personalizing/comparing	Check it out, we all have pluses and minuses
"Shoulds"	Come up with three exceptions

Filtering → Focus on good

Filtering is seen in people with a lot of Fear + Sadness—it starts with self-pity and worsens depression. It is seeing mostly the bad in an Eeyore sort of way instead of seeing any good. At the speaker banquet of life, it's concentrating on the idea that no one remembered the toothpicks for the shrimp instead of seeing the lovely spread of food there. The remedy is to focus on the good: "I'm disappointed but look at all I can still enjoy."

Polarizing, black & white → Think in percents

Black and white thinking is seen in people with Fear + Anger—it's seen especially in the rigid Types. Things and people are all good or all bad, and there's only one way to fix them. At the banquet, it's "the first speaker didn't show, and now the *whole* evening is ruined." The remedy is to think in percents: "The ten-minute speaker didn't show out of our hour meeting so that still leaves 50/60= 83% good enough for me."

Overgeneralizing → No labels; quantify

Overgeneralizing is seen in people with Fear, Anger, Sadness or even Joy—as the perennial optimists do. It's letting one incident or one person make up your mind for the whole group. Racism is a form of overgeneralization. At the banquet, it's thinking, "A man must be in charge. They never remember the details like to call and remind the speakers." The remedy is to concentrate on this one incident and quantify: "Bob fouled this up, but Raul and Cynthia checked on the speakers last time. So Bob is the only man in recent history who didn't confirm with the speakers."

Mind-reading → Ask, no assumptions without words

Mind-reading is seen in people with a lot of Fear + Sadness or Fear + Anger—people who get their feelings hurt easily by taking things personally. At our hypothetical banquet, it's the person sitting in the corner because she's thinking, "Sure, they asked me to join their table, but they didn't really mean it." The remedy is to say, "It looks like you were in the middle of a conversation, and I don't want to intrude." Then we have to take them at their word when they say, "No, come on!"

Catastrophizing ➔ What are the odds
Catastrophizing is pure Fear—it's future-tripping with what could go wrong and playing the "what-if" game. At the speaker banquet, it's thinking, "if that good speaker doesn't show, people are going to leave, and then donations will be down, and then the meeting will have to fold and then I will go out and be homeless." The odds of that cascade of "what-ifs" is close to zero.

Magnifying, can't cope ➔ I can handle it with my HP
Magnifying is Fear of the worse happening in the present or what you just "survived." It is exaggerating the problem and under-estimating our ability to cope with it and then getting overwhelmed. It's saying, "If that construction noise doesn't stop during the banquet, I simply can't take it!" With a few deep breaths and a quick affirmation like, "The problem in front of me is never bigger than the Power behind me," you *can* get through it.

Personalizing/comparing ➔ Check it out, we all have pluses and minuses
Personalizing goes hand in hand with the Fear and Envy that Type 4s have. It is thinking that how others behave is a reflection on something you did. Comparing is seeing how parts of your insides compare with others' outsides, and you judge yourself as better-than or worse-than. It would be like thinking, "These people have been around a lot longer than I have and know so much more that I'm not going to share." The remedy for personalizing is to ask what the other was thinking, as we did for mind-reading. The remedy for the internal comparison game is to tell yourself, "Yes, many of the

people have more time, but they don't have my unique experience—and *that* I can share."

Shoulds → Come up with three exceptions
People with Fear + Anger make up rules on how they and others should behave. I'll digress and share my own story with my very painful "should-ing." I was of the belief that people who litter should be put in stocks and pelted with their own garbage. One morning on my way to work, I stopped to let a woman cross in the crosswalk on the way to the hospital. She was holding the hand of one child and pushing her bald leukemic toddler in the stroller, when she saw some garbage fly off the stroller. Did she drop the hands of her children and run and get it? No, she did not. So three exceptions to my "Thou shalt not litter" rule are 1) you're a parent protecting your kids, 2) you have to get to an important medical appointment because 3) your child has cancer. That was a powerful lesson against my fixed ideas.

Integrating Heart and Head
Our Feelings and our Thoughts are not isolated from each other. One affects the other and is affected in return. Even the research team (cited in Chapter 4) investigating which areas of the brain light up in an MRI found that while there was significant "domain specific correlates" when people engaged in emotions, body feelings, or thoughts, they also found our brains' networks were distributed. This means that while our Feeling networks are concentrated in the limbic system, there are plenty of neural connections to other areas of the brain: our Feelings are connected to our Thoughts and are connected to our Body awareness centers.

The good news is what we already knew—our humanness is indivisible. We are not self-aware when we rely on only one faculty. The hard news is that we can't simply uproot Feelings with our Thoughts, or vice versa. Methods to challenge old ideas or old feelings are a temporary "taking apart" with the final goal of better integration. By first uprooting what's not working, we can connect to both Heart and Head—and Body too—to enrich the enjoyment of our *whole* life.

So dedicate some time to see where your Thoughts are causing you reoccurring trouble. Later we'll examine how to get our Feelings and our Instinctual centers in better balance too.

??? Questions

1. Keep a record of your particular Fixation and Holy Idea. Do you see how you can help share the gift of your Holy Idea with others by manifesting it in your own life?

2. Did you also observe some mental Fixation and Holy Idea coming from your Back-Arrow Type?

3. Every time you are disturbed, pause in the moment or trace it back at the end of the day to which CBT Thought Pattern caused your disturbance. Make it a habit to push out old habits and apply the remedy each and every time. It's not practical to practice the mind-reading remedy on strangers, so make up three alternate explanations to what they could be thinking. Does it diffuse your hot thoughts?

What happened Just the facts	How I evaluated them, My story	Thought Pattern	Remedy Did it help?

CHAPTER 7

BALANCING EMOTIONS: Happy, Joyous and Free

STEP 7
Humbly asked Him to remove our shortcomings.

We are sure God wants us to be happy, joyous, and free. We cannot subscribe to the belief that this life is a vale of tears, though it once was just that for many of us. But it is clear that we made our own misery. God didn't do it. Avoid then, the deliberate manufacture of misery, but if trouble comes, cheerfully capitalize it as an opportunity to demonstrate His omnipotence.[1]

—*Alcoholics Anonymous*

We can call our flaws of under-expression our shortcomings, because they fall short of healthy and compassionate behavior. And we can call our flaws of over-expression our character defects . . . our character defects are normal, healthy things that exceed their proper functions, while our shortcomings are normal, healthy things that aren't reaching their minimal levels of effectiveness.[2]

—Fred H, *Drop the Rock—*
The Ripple Effect

Too Much . . . Too Little

In the last chapter, we examined how our wrong thinking could lead to unhealthy or unnecessarily hurt feelings—or trace the Feelings backward to some self-centered Thought. We already saw what happens when our Ego hijacks our Feeling center, and we act out our defects or Passions. Now we'll check on the Feelings themselves. Our emotions play a vital part in making us who we are. When our Feeling and Thought life are balanced, we experience real emotional maturity. Bill W wrote in *Emotional Sobriety II* that after initial recovery, we need "the development of much more real maturity and balance (which is to say, humility) in our relations with ourselves, with our fellows, and with God."[3] When our Feelings and Thoughts are *not* balanced, we act out in defects or shortcomings.

Fred H in *Drop the Rock—The Ripple Effect* says that one way of defining what our recovery program calls "defects" is what we do too much of while "shortcomings" are what we do too little of.[2] He goes on to say that "Every human being shares the same foundational defect: an **overreliance on self**."[4] The Enneagram shows us how to reduce this overreliance on our Ego constructs. We learn to spot our Passion at work and take steps to move toward our Virtue instead. Another way of experiencing our emotions free of Ego is to see whether our emotions are as balanced as they could be. Our emotions are like the warning lights on our car dashboard; they indicate when something is wrong. So while emotional balance is the desired outcome, emotional upset can be the means of developing insight. Too much or too little access to one of the primary emotions signals we're taking ourselves "too damn seriously."[5] If we're angry almost every time we leave the house, what are our demands? If we don't allow ourselves to feel sad, what are we afraid of? If we're overly or under fearful, aren't we creating the problem we sought to avoid? So let's look at the basic emotions for clues leading to our over- or under-performing behaviors.

Four Basic Emotions

We can use the initial tool of Awareness on our emotions. Different psychologists have added different feelings to the list of four basic emotions below, but we'll concentrate on these four. You can find interesting color wheels representing added feelings, such as "surprise." But surprise could be seen as a combination of Happy + Fear or Angry + Fear, depending on whether it was a pleasant surprise or not. So let's Keep It Simple:

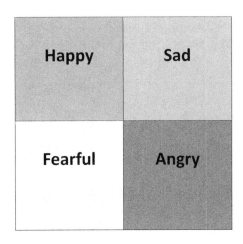

Purpose of Feelings

Feelings are information. They may not be facts, but by paying attention to how we feel when alone or with others, we start to see what makes us tick. The more mature we become, the greater tolerance we have to experience *all* of our feelings. And since they are not facts, our subconscious may trick us by using one feeling to cover up another. If you asked me what I was feeling in early recovery, I would answer: Angry! I kept that same answer for many months until the Steps and people suggested that under all that Anger may be Fear. Yes, indeed. Other people are stuck in Sad or are clinically depressed until they uncover the Anger beneath. Joy can cover Fear; Sadness can cover Joy . . . The cleverest cover-up is how some people (ask your SO4 friend) can use Sadness to cover even deeper Sadness!

These feelings serve a purpose: Anger is to ward off an intrusion or set a boundary. Fear is to keep us safe but not to give us ulcers worrying about what *might* happen. Joy or Happiness propels us toward something, and even Sadness serves a purpose. Researchers at the University of California, Berkeley found that people who were sad were more attuned to details and could remember them more accurately than their happy counterparts.[6] They were better judges whether people were lying to them or not, and being sad was correlated with more perseverance—maybe because that bubbly feeling of happiness makes us more distractible. The fourth and most compelling purpose the researchers found for sadness was that it makes us more empathetic to others. It seems Sadness serves to open us up, or as Leonard Cohen's "Anthem" lyrics say, "There is a crack in everything, that's how the light gets in."[7]

Taking Stock
Giving ourselves permission to feel *all* of our feelings requires a firm tethering to reality: both internal and outer. Emotions are different from emotionalism—what the dictionary defines as "undue indulgence or display of emotion." So while it may be true that inside I am feeling mad, the external "harm" that preceded it could have been fancied. Our maturing selves will pause before mind-reading ourselves into a resentment and ask the other person what was intended, as we practiced in Chapter 6. We need to clarify what is ours, what is theirs and what is our *interpretation* of the situation. This requires self-honesty to catch ourselves telling ourselves "the story" and willingness to consider other possibilities.

Another barrier we may face in allowing our repressed emotions to surface is fear of going into a messy bog of feeling and not being as respected and competent in the world. Rather than rendering us incompetent, firmly acknowledging feelings actually returns self-efficacy. To quote Nathaniel Branden, "To face one's painful emotions . . .

requires courage and honesty; it is not an exercise in self-indulgence. To be self-pitying is to make no effort to deal with one's suffering or to understand it, to complain of it while seeking to avoid confronting it."[8] We take notice of our feelings as information regarding our met or unmet needs. We can use Fear, Anger and Sadness to motivate us away from what's not working and go toward Happiness. This Happiness is not the cheap variety from our pre-recovery days but comes from an examined life—a "new freedom and a new happiness."

Let's take stock of the level of our individual emotions. In the **Questions** section, rate what percentage you have access to the basic emotions—not how much of the time you spend per emotion, but if you were in a situation where most people would feel Happy or Sad or whatever, can you let yourself feel that too? Also note when you might be using one emotion to cover up another—for example, if you're angry at the 98% level, but you can sense there's sadness underneath.

Balancing Our Emotions

Make a plan on how you can redistribute your emotional energy. First, you can decrease doing what you already have too much of. If you're prone to anxiety and watch hours of news that brings up your anxiety—stop. Really. If you watch sad movies or entertain melancholy thoughts enough that it creates an emotional hangover and leaves you less able to act in the world—stop. If you're angry so much of the time that you've made loved ones and yourself miserable—stop. Even happiness can be pathological if it is a way of covering one of the other emotions. There are techniques like Cognitive Behavior Therapy mentioned in Chapter 6 and the **Resources** section to work on your underlying triggers.

You can bring up your low emotions by engaging in music, movies, books, activities and people who bring up those emotions. Low on sadness? Listen to profound music. Not enough anger? How about watching the Rocky movies or practicing with a friend how you'd like to stick up for your needs around a particular coworker? Joy? Hang around with your friends who are lighter and bring out the fun in you—or play more with pets. Fear, well who wants more fear? The point is it's probably under your surface, so you might locate where you're spending energy ignoring it. Pay attention to your Repressed Instinct. If you are Social Instinct Repressed, you can likely spot fear when you meet a group of strangers, but what about when you first see your friends? If you are Sexual or One-to-One Instinct Repressed, let yourself really look into your friend's eyes when you next get together. And if you are Self-Preservation Repressed, go ahead and take care of your security and food/shelter basics and see what your counter-phobia could be covering.

Balance within Our Centers

We might think that all Types within the Feeling center—Types 2, 3 and 4—would easily access their emotions and be able to accomplish emotional balance easily. Riso and Hudson assert that there is over- and under-expression within each of the triads.[9] They found that the first in the triad over-expresses—so Type 2 over-expresses the Heart's Feelings; Type 5 over-expresses the Head's Thinking and Type 8 over-expresses the Body's Instincts.

The second Type within the triad show disconnection from their own center—so Type 3 is cut-off from Feelings; Type 6 from Thoughts and Type 9 from their Instincts. The last Type in the triad under-expresses their center—so Type 4 has trouble with Feelings; Type 7 distracts themselves from Thoughts, and Type 1 represses their Instinctual fire.

This doesn't contradict but rather is a nuance of what we understood before. The Types are still preoccupied and focused on their own center; it's just how they choose to deal with it that is different. For example, a Type 6 person trying *not* to be in his or her Head all the time and using the Body and Feeling centers as an escape, still has a preoccupation with Thinking. Here are possible barriers to fully experiencing all four basic emotions for each of the Types:

Type	Possible Emotional Barriers
1	They may have all of the emotions tamped down because they judge them as not "appropriate." The SP1s and SO1s deny their fear and anger while SX1s acknowledge anger but not fear.
2	Although one of the more emotionally expressive Types, especially the SX2s, SP2s find it hard to express their anger while SO2s repress fear.
3	Type 3s can put on the appropriate emotional mask but often find it hard to connect with their own emotions. SP3s find it hard to connect to happiness; SO3s have difficulty feeling their sadness, and SX3s repress fear.
4	They express emotions well, but SP4s struggle to actually connect with their anger and fear; SO4s with anger and happiness and SX4s use reactive anger to cover their fear and sadness.
5	They can be very emotional underneath but don't like to display emotions. SP5s repress happiness; SO5s repress both fear and happiness, and SX5s repress their anger until it explodes.
6	They are so accustomed to anxious fear yet SX6s deny fear and cover it with anger. SP6s have difficulty feeling their anger, and SO6s have lost touch with both sadness and happiness.
7	The SP7s and SX7s are invested in looking happy most of the time— the SP7s find it hard to admit sadness, and the SX7s repress sadness, fear and anger. The countertype SO7s don't like to show their emotions, especially anger.
8	They seem emotional, but their energy comes from their Instinctual center. SP8s show reactive anger to cover sadness while SO8s and SX8s cover fear.
9	They seem calm but need to reconnect with their own Instinctual center to get in touch with emotions. SP9s have lost touch with happiness and sadness and SO9s and SX9s have lost touch with their healthy anger.

We go into more details on how you can balance across the Head, Body and Heart centers in Chapter 11. For now, we're trying to balance the four major emotions regardless of your Type. The above generalities may not be true for you—we have differences in nature/nurture/will affecting our Type. You know best if you are keeping one or two of the basic emotions repressed. We dissipate our energy by keeping them down and are more resilient for getting in touch with them. Once we are in touch with them, we still get to decide how and with whom to show our reclaimed emotions. What we are striving for is full access to the four basic emotions which make us human.

??? Questions

1. If you have hesitancy to examine your emotional life or bring up your dormant emotions, why could that be?

2. Rate yourself on your access to the basic emotions and make notes on whether you're using them in a healthy way or some dysfunctional way to cover other emotions.

    Sadness   _____%
    Anger   _____%
    Fear   _____%
    Happiness/Joy _____%

3. If you are experiencing any emotions that you use to cover other emotions, how do you plan to not practice them so much? And how will you bring up your lesser-used/lower-access emotions?

CHAPTER 8

THE SHADOW: Making Friends with Our Dark Side

STEP 8
*Made a list of all persons we had harmed,
and became willing to make amends to them all.*

More than most people, the alcoholic leads a double life. He is very much the actor. To the outer world he presents his stage character. This is the one he likes his fellows to see. He wants to enjoy a certain reputation, but knows in his heart he doesn't deserve it.[1]

—*Alcoholics Anonymous*

Unfortunately there can be no doubt that man is, on the whole, less good than he imagines himself or wants to be. Everyone carries a shadow, and the less it is embodied in the individual's conscious life, the blacker and denser it is. If an inferiority is conscious, one always has a chance to correct it. Furthermore, it is constantly in contact with other interests, so that it is continually subjected to modifications. But if it is repressed and isolated from consciousness, it never gets corrected.[2]

—Carl Jung, *Collected Works*
Vol. 11

What is the Shadow?

Carl Jung, the same psychiatrist who told Rowland H he was a hopeless alcoholic unless he could find a "vital spiritual experience,"[3] described the Shadow as the unrecognized, disowned side of ourselves. Jung said, "if [the Shadow] is repressed and isolated from consciousness, it never gets corrected." The shorter version sometimes heard at meetings is, "What we resist—persists."

At the risk of ruining my Type 5 reputation as a deep thinker by referencing Wikipedia, here's what it has to say about our Shadow:

> Because one tends to reject or remain ignorant of the least desirable aspects of one's personality, the shadow is largely negative. There are, however, positive aspects that may also remain hidden in one's shadow (especially in people with low self-esteem, anxieties, and false beliefs).
>
> Carl Jung stated the shadow to be the unknown dark side of the personality. According to Jung, the shadow, in being instinctive and irrational, is prone to psychological projection, in which a perceived personal inferiority is recognized as a perceived moral deficiency in someone else . . . These projections insulate and harm individuals by acting as a constantly thickening veil of illusion between the ego and the real world.[4]

The first paragraph from Wikipedia reminds some people, especially the SO4s and SP9s, that your challenge will be to own all of your positive characteristics. The second paragraph warns us that what we find objectionable in others is what we actually find objectionable in ourselves. We *project* our motives onto others and then get angry or hurt by them. If our aim in Step 8 is to develop "the best possible relations with every human being,"[5] we will have to find a way to stop doing that.

Blocks to Self-Acceptance

Here are possible resistances that each Type might face in seeing their repressed sides:

Type	Resistance to Integrating the Shadow
1	They "should" be good to feel acceptable; their inner critic represses Shadows.
2	They're invested in being seen as optimistic; things could get ugly with the Shadow.
3	The Shadow represents flaws or weaknesses—which are threatening.
4	They value their ability to go to the dark side so their Shadow may be light/good.
5	Any Shadow that limits what their minds can control would make them incapable.
6	They are already scanning for negativity and could feel overwhelmed with more.
7	They habitually focus on the positive, so Shadow work is especially hard for them.
8	Facing and integrating any weakness or neediness will feel vulnerable.
9	Shaky self-value can make them question the need for more dredging of the Ego.

Self-Responsibility

In our recovery program, we've worked hard to become fully functioning members of society again. We may have some fear that accepting our Shadow without shame means condoning it. As we say in meetings—acceptance doesn't mean approval. What seeing our Shadow does is it returns the power of choice to us. We cannot work on what we cannot see. Honestly facing our unconscious desire is not permission to let your inner bank robber loose on the town. Nor is it license to start blurting out all you think to people you know. Shadow work is owning all parts of ourselves, gaining awareness of when we're reacting to someone else because they're doing what our Shadow would like to do but not get caught. Shadow work is largely internal work so that we can be less reactive to others and more accepting of ourselves.

Identifying Our Shadow

The first stage of clearly seeing all parts of ourselves is Awareness of those parts. How do we hear the voice of our Shadow? We've probably all heard or spoken about the committee in our heads. You could clearly name your committee members: Bossy, Poor-me, Scaredy Cat, Lone Wolf . . . Spend time imagining what they are trying to do *for* you, as opposed to only *to* you. I bet many of our committee members have good intentions, not always well phrased. Be especially attuned to the voice of your superego—the critical parental voice—and what its messages are. It may be admonishing your child self in "Why did you do that? You are always so clumsy!" You may not have heard your child self's voice because the critical parent voice was so much louder. Hearing your child self's voice is an essential part of Shadow work because we learned to push down aspects of ourselves as children when we saw they weren't approved of.

There are four exercises in the **Questions** section aimed at uncovering your Shadow with Awareness. While practicing the exercises, remember to keep using Acceptance on what you find or you will only drive the Shadow into hiding again. Remember—rather than make us self-satisfied and resistant to change, Acceptance is actually the precondition to change.

Befriending the Shadow

Why would we want to let these unattractive and repressed urges out of our basement? Well, it takes psychic energy to repress and keep the Shadow down. If we are brave and can face all parts of ourselves, without judgment, we can use that energy to "change the things we can" and use the freed-up energy to live our bigger lives.

Integrating the Shadow fits so well with our 8th Step in recovery because this Step is based on the principle of brotherly and sisterly love. This principle means that we don't see our little plans and designs as more important to us than someone else's are to them. The major work of our 8th Step is not writing the list of persons we had harmed—that could be accomplished in a matter of minutes if we had no psychological resistance. The major work is becoming "willing to make amends to them all." This requires a level of compassion born out of our ability to switch places with that person. There's a famous prayer in the story "Freedom from Bondage" in the Big Book, which has been nicknamed the SOB Prayer. It relies on XA's time-honored tradition of fake it 'til you make it.

> If you have a resentment that you want to be free of . . . Ask for their health, their prosperity, their happiness, and you will be free. Even when you don't really want it for them, and your prayers are only words, and you don't mean it, go ahead and do it anyway. Do it every day for two weeks and you will find you have come to mean it and to want it for them . . . you now feel compassionate understanding and love.[6]

I believe the reason this prayer has the ability to unlock the human heart is that it reminds us of the others' humanity—that they have the same basic needs for health, prosperity and happiness that we do. They probably were grabby and demanding of their desires—and haven't we done the same at different times? I'm referring to the everyday irritations of life and in no way discount deep trauma. Deep trauma may require outside help.

It has been said that when someone irritates us, they're holding up a mirror. "But wait! I would never behave that way." Oh? Yes, we all adopt different strategies to gain love and our place in society, and we're likely to dislike someone who uses an opposite strategy. But often that person who irritates us is using tactics that we would like to use, but we disallow, or we use those same tactics more covertly. In other words, we want to seem like finer human beings but manipulate to get our needs met.

Integrating the Shadow

How do we free up the energy this Shadow is siphoning off? How do we live in more harmony with a greater number of people, including the most tricky of persons, our own relatives? How do we take responsibility for hidden desires and ask straightforwardly for the ones we choose? Like we did with our Type, then our Back-Arrow Type, our Passion and our Instinct:

Awareness — Acceptance — Action

The culmination of finally seeing all parts of ourselves in Awareness, keeping compassion and Acceptance for what we find and moving to the Action stage results in integrating the Shadow. As was said in the Pogo comic strip, "We have met the enemy and he is us." Or, as it says in the *Twelve Steps and Twelve Traditions*, "pride and fear of this sort turn out to be bogeymen, nothing else."[7] We face what we thought was too disgusting in us, we live, and we grow. And maybe along the way, we can forgive more people who are also reactive out of their own Shadow selves.

Shadow Work

Here's a quick and easy way to get started with your own Shadow boxing. Fill out the first question in the **Questions** section. Fill in the blank: I am **not** _____. If I answered quickly off the top of my head, I'd say that I am *not* mean, petty, vain, superficial, stupid . . . Now let me try to own those characteristics. I can be mean, maybe 5% of the time, especially when I'm Hungry, Angry, Lonely or Tired, or with people I judge as trying to exert unfair control over me or people I care about. Petty, vain and superficial? I have these pretty well covered up, but a *small* part of me is jealous of those strutting-through-life types who are so assured of their right to take. It sounds like I have some anger and desire to march in and just take too. Stupid? Well, I'm not stupid—just ignorant of many things. But the fact that I have to tell you that I'm not stupid points to some insecurity that I'm not smart *enough* or that I earn my right to exist through being smart, which is Ego. Try this, and you will find out interesting things about yourself.

Another exercise to try is to look back at your past for key turning points where you felt rejected or that part of you was unacceptable to your parents or important elders. It makes sense that we learn to repress and reject those parts of ourselves that we felt were unacceptable to those we needed to care for us. You will need to process deep trauma with a trained therapist. But for medium-deep work, this visualization can lead to powerful healing. In Question 2, write down incidents from early childhood, middle childhood, late childhood and when you were a teenager. Maybe when you were eight, you heard your parents say, "It's great that Shawn is smart because looks aren't everything." That stung and helps explain why you're overly or under-concerned with your appearance now. Something about your appearance is in your Shadow now because you weren't equipped to fight back then. So find a quiet hour when you can re-visualize these four scenes. But before you replay them, think of someone who can help you champion yourself: a grandparent, an idealized person you made up or perhaps yourself now—older and wiser. Really see that scene when you were put down, using all five senses if you can. Recall the feelings you had and how small you felt to do anything. Then your champion comes in and speaks up, saying just what you needed to hear. Your champion turns to you and lets you speak up. Speak in the language appropriate for your age then. Walk through all four ages, and more if you like. Afterwards, sit quietly for some time to digest what that means and how you have given yourself back the energy and acceptance you didn't receive then. Whew.

The third exercise is similar to our spot-check inventory. It relies on using Gurdjieff's Fourth Way method by observing yourself in your everyday life and consciously choosing greater acceptance. A helpful way of making peace with the idea that you share some of the same traits as the kind of person you dislike is to think in percentages of how much of that trait *you* have. If someone cuts you off on the road, you might think "I can't stand those pushy people who don't care about my safety," for example:

Type who irritates me	Their Behavior	How do I do that?	% of that trait in me
Pushy people	Cut in, act like their needs are more important	Didn't I just go back for something at the supermarket (I wanted to get home) and kept my cart in line? At least I acted nice to the person behind me.	10%

Or if you're usually a tough person and "can't stand those whiny, clingy people," you will find that a small part of you would like to have someone take care of your needs. This opposite side may indeed be a minor component of your whole self, but if you can acknowledge it, you'll find it easier to practice brotherly and sisterly love out in the world.

We are demonstrating to ourselves that we share the same imperious urges as the people who irritate us. We may know this intellectually, but to catch ourselves in the act more frequently will slow down our *projecting* our hidden motives onto them. If we're not afraid of what we'll find within, we gain clarity to call what is ours, what is theirs and what is both of ours. Shadow busting helps us love and understand all the layers we have.

The last exercise is an optional technique for you to try that was developed by Fritz Perls in Gestalt therapy.[8] It's having our regular self who is usually in charge talk to our lesser-seen Shadow side. Once you identify one of your Shadows that is causing you to be reactive, you can hear out what that repressed side has to say. Remember that every behavior has some positive intent—such as to make us safe, bring pleasure or avoid pain. So what that pushy or whiny or whatever Shadow side has to say is something you should hear. You may not choose to act on your Shadow's advice, but hearing it out will calm the internal fight and free up energy. I'm hesitant to suggest that you even switch chairs or talk things over to an empty chair when the two sides are conversing. But we are people who are accustomed to "that committee in our heads," so I trust you won't think I've gone too far.

??? Questions

1. Fill in the blank with as many responses as you can think of. Which of those descriptions come from your identified Ego and which from your Shadow? Is there a small part of you that wants what your Shadow wants?
   I am **not** _____.

2. Visualize key turning points when you felt rejected, and bring in a champion to help you advocate for yourself in:
   Early childhood

   Middle childhood

   Late childhood

   Teenage

3. Fill in the chart over the course of a week noting all the
   types of people who irritate you.

Type who irritates me	Their Behavior	How do I do that?	% of that trait in me

4. Invite one of your Shadows to have a conversation with you
   and really hear out what it has to say. Are there parts of its
   advice that are actually good for you? Did you realize some
   suppressed need?

CHAPTER 9

MANAGING OUR REACTIVITY: Stop It![1] **

STEP 9
*Made direct amends to such people wherever possible,
except when to do so would injure them or others.*

To take inventory in this respect we ought to consider carefully all personal relationships which bring continuous or recurring trouble. It should be remembered that this kind of insecurity may arise in any area where instincts are threatened.[2]

—*Twelve Steps and Twelve Traditions*

As we keep our attention focused on the areas mentioned, and help others do likewise, we establish a flow of communication, back and forth, until compassion manifests naturally: what I am observing, feeling, and needing; what I am requesting to enrich my life; what you are observing, feeling, and needing; what you are requesting to enrich your life.[3]

—Marshall Rosenberg, *Nonviolent Communication*

**Watch the funny/serious skit by Bob Newhart under Note 1 to find out what "Stop It!" means.

Living Amends

If we've been through the Steps a time or two, we have cleared up much of the wreckage and accomplished the major amends. This was hard, no doubt about it. To clear away those guilty-angry feelings, we had to go back to people we harmed and can now live in the 9th Step Promises. The Big Book reminds us that forgiveness is a two-way street—the more we can stop blaming others, the more we're able to forgive ourselves. "[X]A has taught me that I will have peace of mind in exact proportion to the peace of mind I bring into the lives of other people."[4] But certainly we are not saints now. People still irritate us and often the same *type* of people. Even after years of recovery, we can find that we have the same old buttons pushed by the same old type of people with different faces.

The Enneagram, with its deep psychological insights, can help free us more. Instead of living plateaued out, what if we could live in harmony with people, places and things most of the time? We know the spiritual tools to acceptance: prayer, meetings, talking with another person in recovery, writing inventories, service . . . But we can *still* step on the toes of our fellows, and they retaliate.

Here's how the *Twelve Steps and Twelve Traditions* defines "harm": "To define the word 'harm' in a practical way, we might call it the result of instincts in collision, which cause physical, mental, emotional, or spiritual damage to people."[5]

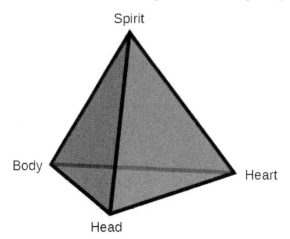

Both the Twelve Steps and the Enneagram emphasize how important the three parts are—our Body, Heart and Head. If we imagine our three aspects of Body, Heart and Head as suspended in a child's mobile and allow our HP/Spirit/Essence to pull us up—our three aspects will become balanced and in harmony. This is critical within us and critical to remember when we are dealing with others. They, too, have the Body, Heart, Head and Spirit trying to have all needs met and stay in balance. Our living amends depends on finding and using new tools to get along more harmoniously.

Minimizing Reactivity

Reactivity is when our feelings and interpretations are overly determined by outside events instead of staying centered. When our five senses take in information and what we observe doesn't affect our Ego's soft spot—there's no big reaction. But, as Ken Wilber wrote in *Meeting the Shadow*, "Projection on the Ego Level is very easily identified: if a person or thing in the environment *informs* us, we probably aren't projecting; on the other hand, if it *affects* us, chances are that we are a victim of our own projections."[6] Wilber provides the example of a man who wanted to and also didn't want to clean the garage. When his wife asked him how he was progressing, he snapped at her because he was at war with his own conscience. He was projecting his nagging voice inside himself onto his wife. As the *Twelve Steps and Twelve Traditions* puts it, "It is a spiritual axiom that every time we are disturbed, no matter what the cause, there is something wrong *with us*."[7]

Our lives will be cleaner, more harmonious and satisfying if we can find psychological tools to augment our spiritual tools to live life on life's terms. In Chapter 8, we found out about our Shadows. The more we can see our common need in the person who offended us, the more we can integrate that side of the "Other" into ourselves. The Enneagram map teaches us to leave our home Type to gather new perspectives, and bring them home to integrate them. When we have integrated many of the other Types into our toolkit, the number of people in the "Other" category is much less and fewer people stand in the way of our having a great day. In the last chapter, we practiced this process:

Awareness — Acceptance — Action

As was said in the Introduction, "Personality change involves Awareness of what's not working; Acceptance that when we try on new behavior, we're likely to overshoot the mark or do the new behavior awkwardly at first; and finally Action— putting new behaviors into day-to-day practice and modifying them once we see how they work." The Acceptance stage comes with mourning as we figure out that we were not as right, and the "Other" was not as wrong. It's sad that we could be trapped in our limited way of seeing things for so long, and it will take Action to make lasting changes.

The Action step of better relations with people around us requires connecting to them with our similarities rather than our differences. When we first came into this strange world of recovery and may have wanted to run, we were told to "Look for the similarities, not the differences." Step 8 in the *Twelve Steps and Twelve Traditions* says, "Learning how to live in the greatest peace, partnership, and brotherhood with all men and women, of whatever description, is a moving and fascinating adventure."[8] *I'd say.* Let's see how we can see that shining heart in another, even in those we initially don't like.

Nonviolent Communication

Nonviolent Communication (NVC), while not part of the Enneagram system, helps us minimize our reactivity and form better relationships with all people. It is a technique to bring warring factions, sparring partners and regular day-to-day interactions together through seeing our mutual needs and feelings. If this sounds sugary and too-good-to-be-true, watch Marshall Rosenberg's video (see **Resources**). This technique that he pioneered helped bring years of conflict to an end and can be used equally well at your next family or work function.

Try NVC out first at home with your loved ones, and once you gain ability with the basics, start to use it whenever you feel an impasse. What's more, NVC isn't only to keep interactions nonviolent but can be used on ourselves for better awareness and compassion. NVC even adds meaning to compliments by shifting focus from our favorable judgment of another to what they did that enriched our life.

Four components of NVC
(Adapted from Marshall Rosenberg's *Nonviolent Communication*[9])

1. Observations— concrete actions or data that a video camera would record—so no interpretive words like "When you say such <u>judgmental</u> things." Say instead, "When you said that my piano playing was like a two-year old's."

2. Feelings—How we feel about what we observe (see Feelings list)
To distinguish feelings from thoughts, avoid "I feel that <u>you</u> . . ." and what we think others are thinking about us. Instead of "I feel put down," keep the focus only on our feelings: "I feel angry and disturbed."

3. Needs—our values and desires that are/are not met (see Needs list)

4. Requests—concrete actions that we request—again, something that a video camera would record—so not "Please listen to me when I'm speaking" (because how can you prove that the other person did indeed listen?) but "Could we turn off the TV, and you tell me what you just heard me say?" Requests should be for what we *do* want rather than what we don't want. And the difference between a request and a demand means no bad attitude if the person says "No." We can renegotiate but not manipulate the other person into giving us what we want. We can try to have our needs met

elsewhere or in a different way. The whole point of NVC is:

Satisfaction for both sides — Not compromise

NVC Format
1. When I see/hear_____
2. I feel_____ because
3. My need for_____ is/isn't met.
4. Would you_____?

The wonderful thing about seeing needs and feelings in every interaction is if we can spot them in ourselves, we can spot them in others and *vice-versa*. If we're feeling bad in some situation, we can pause and look for our need that isn't getting met. If we are shut-down and don't want to listen to what another person says, by extending compassion to ourselves first, it softens that hard protective stance against the other. For example, suppose the big boss at work is holding a meeting and doesn't seem remotely interested in your unique contributions or how hard you worked on a project. In that case, you could do an internal inventory like "She's pushing us pretty hard, she may have the board breathing down her neck. Right now, I don't even care. Hmmm, it seems my needs for inclusion, mutual respect and effectiveness are not getting met. She's 'including us' by telling us what's going to happen in this meeting but not in an equal sense. Yes, she's the boss. For 'mutual respect' I can affirm that as a person, I am entitled to the same respect for my humanity that she is. Now 'effectiveness or agency' I can do something about. I'm not going to say anything in front of hundreds of people now. Still, when she attends our departmental meeting in two days, I could say something like, 'When you said that our project has to launch in four weeks and would no longer include what our group worked on, I felt disturbed because my need to trust in the timeline agreed upon was not met and I felt discouraged because I have a need for agency. Could you explain why the timeline was moved up and why our group's contributions were eliminated?'" This is respectful and restores our sense that we spoke up for ourselves.

Advanced level NVC involves guessing and asking what the other needs. It means staying responsive to the fact that the other person has needs, even if unexpressed or expressed negatively. Let's say you arrive home and your partner is in a snappish mood. Something went wrong at last night's barbecue, but you were both tired and went to bed. After a few more cupboards get slammed,

> You say, "Last night I made a joke that you could get lost in a broom closet. Did you feel hurt and angry because you have a need for respect?"
>
> He replies, "I wasn't hurt. Forget about it."
>
> You might say, "So you weren't hurt, but there's something going on. Was it your need for confidence about driving that matters to you?"
>
> He says, "No, I just don't like you running me down in front of our friends."
>
> You: "You're feeling angry because your need for competence in front of others wasn't met?"
>
> He says: "Sort of. I know I get lost a lot—my family used to make fun of me for that. It's just that Lou was there and he's always one-upping me. I can't stand that."
>
> You: "You felt self-conscious because your need for equality with Lou was messed with, and you felt upset with me because your need for partnership and support wasn't met?"
>
> He says: "Yes about the support from you part. No, I didn't feel self-conscious about Lou but angry. Yeah, I'm angry at him and taking it out on you."
>
> You: "Got it. You would like my support of you as my partner, and you're angry at Lou because your need for respect from him isn't met. Right?"

He says: "That's pretty much it, thanks for understanding."

It sounds like a lot of work and perhaps codependent to try to figure out what someone else is feeling and needing. But when we can focus on what's underneath, we can experience our common humanity. When we hear that someone has a need that we share, there's a bridge toward common solutions. When we can see our feelings separate from our judgments, we are less likely to be manipulated by others' emotions—we spot when feelings are misinterpreted as facts. NVC helps balance our Body-Heart-Head centers by getting us to take responsibility for our own feelings, see when our thoughts and interpretations of events cause us pain and ask for what we would like in a straightforward manner.

Nonviolent communication is not the only method to develop our emotional intelligence. In fact, NVC is not part of the Enneagram practice—lowering our reactivity is. Search out a different method if you prefer and then practice it in your home and then outside the home for a while. This approach works to improve communication with people of all Types—with people in the Instinctual Body center because it helps diffuse their anger when their needs are heard and they feel respected. It helps with people in the Feeling center because both sides are getting clear about their own feelings and not pushing them onto someone else. NVC creates a wonderful bridge to people in the Head center too because the needs sound rational, everyone has needs, and it helps them to get to their feelings. This will be a step toward amending old patterns with people and mending the thought patterns that cause *us* reoccurring pain.

Needs and Feelings Inventories
(c) 2005 by Center for Nonviolent Communication

Needs Inventory[10]

CONNECTION
acceptance
affection
appreciation
belonging
cooperation
communication
closeness
community
companionship
compassion
consideration
consistency
empathy
inclusion
intimacy
love
mutuality
nurturing
respect/self-respect

CONNECTION continued
safety
security
stability
support
to know and be known
to see and be seen
to understand and be understood
trust
warmth

PHYSICAL WELL-BEING
air
food
movement/exercise
rest/sleep
sexual expression
safety
shelter
touch
water

HONESTY
authenticity
integrity
presence

PLAY
joy
humor

PEACE
beauty
communion
ease
equality
harmony
inspiration
order

AUTONOMY
choice
freedom
independence
space
spontaneity

MEANING
awareness
celebration of life
challenge
clarity
competence
consciousness
contribution
creativity
discovery
efficacy
effectiveness
growth
hope
learning
mourning
participation
purpose
self-expression
stimulation
to matter
understanding

Feelings- When Our Needs <u>Are</u> Satisfied[11]

AFFECTIONATE
compassionate
friendly
loving
open hearted
sympathetic
tender
warm

ENGAGED
absorbed
alert
curious
engrossed
enchanted
entranced
fascinated
interested
intrigued
involved
spellbound
stimulated

HOPEFUL
expectant
encouraged
optimistic

CONFIDENT
empowered
open
proud
safe
secure

EXCITED
amazed
animated
ardent
aroused
astonished
dazzled
eager
energetic
enthusiastic
giddy
invigorated
lively
passionate
surprised
vibrant

GRATEFUL
appreciative
moved
thankful
touched

INSPIRED
amazed
awed
wonder

JOYFUL
amused
delighted
glad
happy
jubilant
pleased
tickled

EXHILARATED
blissful
ecstatic
elated
enthralled
exuberant
radiant
rapturous
thrilled

PEACEFUL
calm
clear headed
comfortable
centered
content
equanimous
fulfilled
mellow
quiet
relaxed
relieved
satisfied
serene
still
tranquil
trusting

REFRESHED
enlivened
rejuvenated
renewed
rested
restored
revived

Feelings- When Our Needs Are <u>Not</u> Satisfied

AFRAID
apprehensive
frightened
mistrustful
panicked
scared
suspicious
terrified
wary
worried

ANNOYED
aggravated
dismayed
disgruntled
displeased
exasperated
frustrated
impatient
irritated
irked

ANGRY
enraged
furious
indignant
irate
outraged
resentful

AVERSION
appalled
contempt
disgusted
dislike
hate
horrified
hostile
repulsed

CONFUSED
ambivalent
baffled
bewildered
dazed
hesitant
lost
mystified
puzzled
torn

DISCONNECTED
alienated
aloof
apathetic
bored
cold
detached
distant
indifferent
numb
withdrawn

DISQUIET
agitated
alarmed
discombobulated
disconcerted
disturbed
perturbed
rattled
restless
shocked
startled
surprised
troubled
uncomfortable
uneasy
unnerved

EMBARRASSED
ashamed
chagrined
flustered
guilty
mortified
self-conscious

FATIGUE
beat
burnt out
depleted
exhausted
lethargic
listless
sleepy
tired
worn out

PAIN
agony
devastated
grief
heartbroken
hurt
lonely
miserable
regretful
remorseful

SAD
depressed
despair
despondent
disappointed
discouraged
disheartened
forlorn
hopeless

TENSE
anxious
cranky
distressed
distraught
edgy
fidgety
frazzled
irritable
jittery
nervous
overwhelmed
restless
stressed out

VULNERABLE
fragile
guarded
helpless
insecure
leery
reserved
sensitive
shaky

YEARNING
envious
jealous
longing
nostalgic
pining
wistful

??? Questions

1. Practice NVC just inside your head for a few days. Whenever you're disturbed, take a breath and say to yourself, "I'm feeling _____ because my need for _____ is not met." If you have two or more different feelings, find a separate unmet need for each. Does this help diffuse your reaction?

2. Practice NVC (or another emotional intelligence technique) with someone you trust for a week. NVC is also great for giving more meaningful compliments because it acknowledges what *they did* instead of putting our judgment, however positive, on them. Did this clarify what your own needs and feelings were? Did it change any patterns of interactions with your trusted person?

3. Practice NVC out in the world. Did it help to see the needs and feelings underneath someone else's behavior? Did it change your interactions?

CHAPTER 10

OUR WINGS: For Added Balance

STEP 10
*Continued to take personal inventory
and when we were wrong promptly admitted it.*

Our inventory allows us to settle with the past. When this is done, we are really able to leave it behind us. When our inventory is carefully taken, and we have made peace with ourselves, the conviction follows that tomorrow's challenges can be met as they come.[1]

—*Twelve Steps and Twelve Traditions*

Your basic type dominates your overall personality, while the wing complements it and adds important, sometimes contradictory, elements to your total personality . . . Moreover, everyone has both wings in the sense that to some extent we all have all nine types in our personality.[2]

—Don Richard Riso and Russ Hudson,
Personality Types

The Wings Offer Balance

Becoming aware and using traits from our Arrows is hard work. Adopting strengths from our neighboring Wings should feel relatively easy, at least for one of your Wings. The Wings are the Types on both sides of your home Type moving *around* the circle of the Enneagram, not via the inner lines. So Wings for Type 6 would be Types 5 and 7; for Type 9 would be Types 8 and 1, etc. If you look back to your Enneagram Quiz results, likely one of your Wings has a much higher score than the other. Adopting these traits will be like visiting your friend while work toward adopting the less developed Wing will feel more like—well, work.

They offer us balance by providing us access to more ways of looking at the world and responding to it. At least one of your Wings will necessarily be within your same center of Body, Heart or Head intelligence. You might expect that Wing to be your more developed one, but it's not a given. So we'll integrate whichever is your more accessible Wing first and then work on appreciating and developing traits from the other side. Like a bird or plane with one wing with greater lift, we would fly in circles if our Wings are not balanced!

Stronger Wing

Reread **Passions to Virtues per Type** in Chapter 2 for your stronger Wing. Are you already practicing those traits, at least part of the time? For a more precise description of what our Virtues look like, we'll need to look at Subtype. Recall that as we move around the dynamic Enneagram, we keep a definite preference for keeping our same Instinctual Sequence. Keep your same Dominant Instinct in mind as you reread the **Subtype Summary** in Chapter 5 for your stronger Wing. Does this Instinctual Subtype sound the closest, or does another? We'll spend a shorter time practicing becoming aware of and integrating the stronger Wing's traits in the **Questions** section at the end of the chapter.

If your stronger Wing is in a different center than your own, how do you already use these traits? Let's say you're a

Type 1 in the Body center of intelligence, and your Wing Type 2 (1w2) is in the Heart center. Initially, you are likely to "feel" your feelings Instinctually and instantly in your Body. See if you can get in touch with your pure feelings. Similarly, if you're a Type 5 with a Type 4 Wing (5w4), you will tend to think your "feelings" for a while and will need to check in with your real feelings. Talk this over with your Feelings-first friends and you'll see the distinction.

The same increased awareness happens for Type 7 with an 8 Wing (7w8) who gains access to gut-level Body reactions from visiting the Body center from the Head center—they may use their Bodies to escape from their dominant function of thinking. Likewise, Type 2s with a Type 1 Wing will approach the Instinctual center from their Feelings-first preference.

Neighboring Types to the Head center will still lead with their dominant center. Type 4w5s can seem cerebral, but their feelings are informing them first. Type 8w7's robust Instinctual center will predominate over their cerebral studiousness.

Wing Types

When Don Riso and Russ Hudson wrote *Personality Types* in 1996, they developed the concept of Wings to account for variability seen between people of the same Type. Further discoveries in the ever-growing understanding within the Enneagram community regard the Instincts combining with the Type's Passion forming Subtype as more potent predictors of behavior and better indicators toward optimal personal growth. Nevertheless, our stronger Wing colors our personality, aids in identification within the Enneagram system, and offers a broader range of life perception. Here is a brief summary of Wings adapted from *Personality Types*[3]:

~~~~~~

The 18 Wing Types

TYPE 1w9 "The Idealist"- Type 1s are similar to Type 9s by both being somewhat removed from real life—but the dissatisfaction Type 1s experience from people not behaving "correctly" is at odds with Type 9's desire to get along. They are idealistic, logical and scholarly—often using their gift to educate and uplift others. They can become so removed from everyday reality that they can seem reclusive and harshly judgmental at lower levels of development. Famous 1w9s include Al Gore, CS Lewis and Sandra Day O'Connor.

TYPE 1w2 "The Advocate"- Both Types are trying to be good: Type 1s to fulfill their moral imperative and Type 2s to win appreciation and love. Type 2 softens the rigidity of Type 1, and so 1w2s work well with others for social causes. At lower levels, the desire for self-control from Type 1 combusts with the desire to control others from Type 2, and they can become overly instructive. Famous 1w2s include Mahatma Gandhi, Margaret Thatcher and Ralph Nader.

TYPE 2w1 "The Servant"- Type 1's almost opposite strategy adds a sense of duty and rationality to the Type 2's emotionalism. While still trying to be the Helper, Type 2w1s will help because it's the principled and right thing to do, sometimes despite their feelings. The Perfectionism lent them from their Type 1 Wing can compel them to serve out of a sense of guilt over "all that they have." Famous 2w1s include Desmond Tutu, Mother Theresa and Lewis Carroll.

TYPE 2w3 "The Host/Hostess"- The two Types are within the Feeling center, and they reinforce each other. Type 2's seeking love through helping others will be done with even more charm and self-assurance. Their giving has an open-heartedness lent them from Type 3's enjoyment of life and appreciation of themselves. They work hard to secure Type 2's need for recognition, and Type 3's need to be seen as desirable—and are prone to jealousy. Famous 2w3s include Luciano Pavarotti, Barbara Bush and John Denver.

TYPE 3w2 "The Star"- Again, the two Types within the same Feeling center reinforce each other, but since Type 3 is dominant, 3w2s are more direct about what they want. The Type 2 Wing allows the more reserved and poised Type 3 to show more feelings—sometimes strategically. Actors are prevalent in this Type, and the obsession to be liked and admired can make them divas and even narcissistic at the lower levels. Famous 3w2s include Bill Clinton, Shirley MacLaine and Whitney Houston.

TYPE 3w4 "The Professional"- The outgoing nature of Type 3 opposes the inward-drawing nature from Type 4, resulting in a more subdued, private but still artistic personality. Type 4 lends emotional awareness, and so 3w4s have greater access to their feelings *and* having them hurt. The Wing adds intellectual depth as well, and they value rational solutions to getting tasks done with style. At lower levels, they can waver between the over-confidence from Type 3 and self-doubt from Type 4. Famous 3w4s include Meryl Streep, Sting and Bryant Gumbel.

TYPE 4w3 "The Aristocrat"- As for the 3w4s, two different motivations contradict each other in the 4w3s. The Type 4's naturally introverted nature and focus on authenticity is forced outward with Type 3's extroversion and demand for attention. This can help Type 4 to be more action-oriented, social and ambitious. Craving success and yet fear of failing can make them duplicitous or emotionally fake at lower levels. Famous 4w3s include Rudolf Nureyev, Judy Garland and Albert Camus.

TYPE 4w5 "The Bohemian"- Both Types are introverted and introspective—Type 4 with their feelings and Type 5 with their thoughts—making the 4w5s intense and profoundly creative people. Type 5 reduces the social insecurity Type 4s experience. Their work is original, even unusual, but they can still feel isolated socially. At lower levels, too much turning inward can cause emotional turmoil. Famous 4w5s include Edgar Allan Poe, Anne Rice and Johnny Depp.

TYPE 5w4 "The Iconoclast"- Types 5 and 4 reinforce each other so that 5w4s are drawn to the internal landscape to synthesize new ideas with creativity. Their thinking is more intuitive than purely analytical, as it tends to be for the other Wing. For them, Truth is Beauty. They can become so isolated in thoughts and macabre feelings that they can be nihilistic and have crises of meaning at their lower levels. Famous 5w4s include Albert Einstein, Georgia O'Keeffe and Tim Burton.

TYPE 5w6 "The Problem Solver"- Since both Types are in the Thinking triad, they amplify using their minds to solve life's problems and are highly analytical. Type 6 lends practicality but also anxiety to Type 5 and leaves 5w6s cut off from emotions. Type 6 loyalty makes them want to participate in social structures more but in an admittedly socially nerdy way. Fear at their lower levels can make them argumentative and anti-authoritarian. Famous 5w6s include Stephen Hawking, Simone Weil and Bill Gates.

TYPE 6w5 "The Defender"- Although both in the Thinking center, Type 6's goal of joining with others is at odds with Type 5's detaching style. Looking for alliances while not trusting others makes them defenders of the little guy against the system. They are the practical intellectuals who excel within organizations with set parameters. At unhealthy levels, the secretiveness from Type 5 adds to the suspicion of Type 6, leaving them paranoid. Famous 6w5s include Malcolm X, Michelle Pfeiffer and Phil Donahue.

TYPE 6w7 "The Buddy"- The traits from Type 7 for gregariousness reinforce loyal joining tendencies from Type 6 and magnify the desire for affiliation. But the native Type 6 fear makes them monitor others' reactions to check if they are accepted. The 6w7 is friendly, humorous and hardworking. Type 7's future planning can make their fear worse about the future, and they can alternate between staying in unhealthy work or personal relations and becoming reckless. Famous 6w7s include Johnny Carson, Jay Leno and Reggie Jackson.

TYPE 7w6 "The Entertainer"- Type 6 seeks safety through affiliation with others while Type 7 looks toward things out in the environment, creating some tension in the 6w7. Still, the gregariousness from Type 7 and the determination from Type 6 make for a generally successful, outgoing person with a keen wit. At lower levels, the restlessness from Type 7 combines with suspicion from Type 6, and they can be erratic and demanding. Famous 7w6s include Robin Williams, Bette Midler and Marianne Williamson.

TYPE 7w8 "The Realist"- Type 7's going for what they want gets amplified from Type 8s projecting themselves upon their environment, making for an assertive and even aggressive Type. They are active, intense; work hard and play hard. They work for and enjoy material things, including expensive toys. They can go to extremes and engage in risky behavior at lower levels. Famous 7w8s include John F Kennedy, Larry King and Lauren Bacall.

TYPE 8w7 "Maverick"- Type 8s seeking power and autonomy is reinforced by Type 7s seeking novel experiences to make them straightforward, adventurous people who don't allow opposition to slow them down. The joy of living from Type 7 adds charisma to the leadership qualities from Type 8, and they are natural entrepreneurs. They can browbeat others when trying to protect their position and lash out as bullies at the lower levels. Famous 8w7s include Lee Iacocca, Barbara Walters and Muhammad Ali.

TYPE 8w9 "The Bear"- Type 8's need for power is softened by Type 9's need for peace, but 8w9s are still forces of nature. Their name "Bear" indicates their protectiveness of their close people, and they will aggressively defend them. This aggressiveness can turn vengeful at lower levels of development. Famous 8w9s include Martin Luther King, Jr, Janet Reno and Johnny Cash.

TYPE 9w8 "The Comfort Seeker"- Type 9's comfort-seeking plus Type 8's persuasiveness adds an edge of physicality. Type 8 lends extroversion so that 9w8s do well in business where they can channel their helping capacity. They seem earthy and calm until someone interferes with their well-being, and then they can explode. Famous 9w8s include Kevin Costner, Sophia Loren and Keanu Reeves.

TYPE 9w1 "The Dreamer"- Both Types repress their emotions, especially anger. Type 1's idealism adds to Type 9's peacekeeping tendencies making them principled, fair and philosophical. Type 1 adds objectivity, so 9w1s are good mediators or therapists and can bring in different schools of thought. Their anger can erupt if they judge others as doing something unfair. Famous 9w1s include Carl Jung, Queen Elizabeth II and Walt Disney.

~~~~~~

Weaker Wing
Reread **Passions to Virtues per Type** in Chapter 2 for your weaker Wing. What traits attract you, and what traits are you apathetic toward? Are there disowned traits from your Shadow? If there is a definite dislike for these traits, you have turned off access to the Virtues of your weaker Wing and will

need to work through this if you'd like **MORE**. Here is what your less developed Wing has to offer your Type:

TYPE 1
Weaker Wing Type 9- Type 9 will allow you to "mellow out" and relax some of your black and white thinking in Peacekeeping by seeing another point of view as valid too— increasing your Serenity.

Weaker Wing Type 2- By striving to be a Helper, you can get out of your "bondage of self" by developing compassion for others *and* yourself.

TYPE 2
Weaker Wing Type 1- Type 1s know who they are, and this inner compass can help balance out giving too much of yourself away, making you a better Helper for yourself and then others.

Weaker Wing Type 3- Type 3's more overt desire to look and perform well can bring some of your hidden desires for the same out of the Shadow.

TYPE 3
Weaker Wing Type 2- Type 3s can compartmentalize feelings, and Type 2 will give ready access to feelings—making you a more complete and competent total person.

Weaker Wing Type 4- Type 4 is determined to fight for authenticity, a virtue that Type 3 can use to leave behind Self-Deceit for Veracity.

TYPE 4
Weaker Wing Type 3- Type 3s get the job done—they focus on their task and don't get bogged down in feelings. If you can borrow from their persona, it will lead to real self-esteem and the ability to savor your accomplishments.

Weaker Wing Type 5- Type 5s are in their Heads, and balancing your emotional intelligence with the ability to analyze and discriminate will allow you to deepen your understanding of the world.

TYPE 5

Weaker Wing Type 4- Mixing in a more intuitive understanding from Type 4 will allow your mental steps to take leaps and go much further than a strictly methodological approach.

Weaker Wing Type 6- Type 6's more practical approach to life can alleviate some of the heaviness from being "deep" so much of the time.

TYPE 6

Weaker Wing Type 5- Type 5s are not afraid to stand alone in their opinions—which can alleviate your need to check your thoughts against others and allow a more novel approach.

Weaker Wing Type 7- Type 7s are fun. They bring back an element of play and spontaneity that will allow you to recharge your batteries.

TYPE 7

Weaker Wing Type 6- Type 6s have a more cautious approach that will help you slow down and focus your energies. They bring the enjoyment of camaraderie that will help you join in and enjoy life more.

Weaker Wing Type 8- Type 8s are a force of nature that can counteract hiding out in the group and let you further *your* values and objectives. Their crisp, businesslike approach allows you to be more straightforward and bring your projects to completion.

TYPE 8

Weaker Wing Type 7- Type 7s lend some agreeableness for getting along with others while still allowing you to further your goals—with a little time left over for fun and adventure.

Weaker Wing Type 9- Type 9s help balance out striving with greater acceptance of life's obstacles to take things a bit easier.

TYPE 9

Weaker Wing Type 8- Type 8's focus on practical matters helps bring you down to earth and enjoy all that being more in your Body can bring.

Weaker Wing Type 1- Type 1s expand your ability from making a mark in the world to make time to enlarge your spiritual life.

~~~~~~

??? Questions

1. Did your Wing Type give you further information about how you see and behave in the world? What do you like in yourself that seems a combination between your home Type and your stronger Wing?

2. What does your stronger Wing offer you? Which traits do you enjoy having access to that your home Type doesn't provide? Keep a log for a short while focusing awareness on when you use these traits and see if you can develop them more.

3. What does your weaker Wing offer you? If you have actively turned away from using the high side Virtues of this Wing, what might you be repressing or afraid of? Do you have friends, or could you make friends with people of this Type? In your log, pay attention to instances when you could use these traits and see if you can develop them more. What did you learn from this?

CHAPTER 11

BODY-HEART-HEAD: In Harmony

STEP 11
Sought through prayer and meditation to improve our conscious contact with God <u>as we understood Him,</u> praying only for knowledge of His will for us and the power to carry that out.

Those of us who have come to make regular use of prayer would no more do without it than we would refuse air, food, or sunshine. And for the same reason. When we refuse air, light, or food, the body suffers. And when we turn away from meditation and prayer, we likewise deprive our minds, our emotions, and our intuitions of vitally needed support. As the body can fail its purpose for lack of nourishment, so can the soul.[1]

—Twelve Steps and Twelve Traditions

We are programmed from early childhood to believe that we need to be better, to try harder, and to discount parts of ourselves that other parts do not approve of. The whole of our culture and education constantly reminds us of how we can be more successful, desirable, secure, or spiritual if we were only to change in some way or other. In short, we have learned that we need to be different from how we actually are according to some formula the mind has received. The idea that we simply need to discover and accept who we actually are is contrary to almost everything we have been taught.[2]

—Don Riso and Russ Hudson,
The Wisdom of the Enneagram

Improve Our Contact

Since we've been in recovery, we have probably crafted a prayer and meditation life that
works for us. We may still be searching for a meditation practice more suited to us, but people in recovery can rarely be accused of "spiritual bypass"—not doing the spiritual work. We worked because our lives depended on it. If psycho-spiritual development relies on both psychological and spiritual growth, then chances are we can focus on psychological aspects to balance our Bodies-Hearts and Heads.

Balancing Across Centers

We've balanced our feelings by redistributing energy from the low-side of Passions to the high-side of Virtues in Chapters 2, 3 and 10; we're working on bringing up the lesser-used emotions in Chapter 7 and decreased our emotional reactivity in Chapter 9. We applied the same process of **Awareness—Acceptance—Action** to bring more of our Head-based Fixations into harmony with our Holy Ideas in Chapter 6. We've even brought traits from previously ignored Types into the light from our Shadow side in Chapter 8. Our final work before moving forward is to balance the Body-Heart and Head centers not *within* but *across* the three centers. In other words, we may have balanced our Feelings to have similar access to Fear, Anger, Sadness and Happiness, but the greater need is to pay more attention to the Body now, for example.

You might think that all Types within the Instinctual triad of Types 8, 9 and 1 would have mastered kinesthetic intelligence; Feeling triad Types 2, 3 and 4 would have mastered emotional intelligence and Thought triad Types 5, 6 and 7 would have mastered cognitive intelligence. But often the Types right in the middle of their center of intelligence—Types 3, 6 and 9—struggle with their own center. Type 3 people actually push their feelings aside to make the fastest progress in their careers. Type 6s escape into their Bodies and Feelings to avoid the Fear in their minds. And Type 9s can go to sleep to their own Bodies' needs and get lost in feelings or their minds.[3] Each of the Types displays a deficit in one of the centers of intelligence and can benefit from extra work in that area. This time we'll start with Type 8 in the Body center:

Type	Increase	Specific Work Needed
8	Heart	Open the heart to softer, more vulnerable interactions.
9	Body	Stay grounded in your body and trust Instincts more.
1	Head	Meditate on Serenity and become aware of repressed Anger.
2	Head	Read and meditate on Humility; take responsibility for own needs.
3	Heart	Open your heart to explore covered inferiority and admit errors.
4	Body	Feel what a strong container your body is and stay grounded.
5	Body	Get grounded in your body instead of lost in obsessive thoughts.
6	Head	Meditate on Faith and Courage; see when you're projecting fear.
7	Heart	Face and release the sadness to really be open to life.

Body Work

Because our bodies are so foundational to our existence, we all need to move our bodies for healthy emotions and thoughts. The low in body awareness Types—Types 4, 5 and 9—can especially benefit. We may intellectually know this but push daily exercise off as something "we'll get around to." We know we'll feel better but . . . the sock drawer needs organizing. To quote a shoe campaign, "Just Do It!" We can add a day or two per week to whatever routine we currently have and even balance two of our aspects at once. People with the Social Instinct dominant can add a day of lone exercise while Social Instinct repressed folk can join a class. Try...

Besides moving our bodies, we can become more aware of our body states throughout the day. By scanning our bodies from head to toe when we are in the middle of some situation, we'll become aware of where we hold our anxiety, joy, anger and hurt feelings. We can acknowledge feelings and either "accept the things we cannot change" or "change the things we can." Identify the three areas of your body where you hold the most tension. Then try a three breath mini-meditation a few times during the day when you breathe into these three areas and relax them. And don't forget a positive body scan. Usually, we can feel what's not right in our bodies first—but go back from head to toe and find what's right. There are pleasant sights, sounds, smells, tastes and sensations—both internal and external. By taking extra seconds to savor them, we can increase our well-being.

We can use the cues from our body-center as prods toward action. If we're anxious, we may need to put down that narcotizing activity and get into Right Action, Type 9's Virtue. The body provides prods *toward* activities too when we can reinterpret nervousness for anticipation, for example. There are times when time flies when we are just *being*, and we can delight in "the flow."[4] The high in body awareness Types are especially good in this kinesthetic awareness but we can all cultivate this sense.

Then we can benefit from receiving body work from professionals. Try a couple of new experiences of massage or Reiki, Kundalini, Qigong, Feldenkrais to sky-diving. Being alive in our bodies makes us happy, like a pup bounding across a meadow.

Emotions Work

We have already covered the key points that we all need to develop in order to lead emotionally sober lives. Emotional

Intelligence starts with Awareness regarding our own emotional patterns and handicaps, in the form of our Passions. This Awareness stage merges into Acceptance when we identify our "hot-thoughts" leading to emotional volatility and reactivity. We needed further Awareness and Acceptance to see how we project our own disowned traits from our Shadow onto others. We began to get into the solution of the Action stage of personal development when we focused on our needs and feelings and how they were similar to others' needs and feelings. Now we are working on the last of the four key points toward raising our Emotional IQ—we're cultivating healthier relationships based on emotional authenticity.

Emotional IQ	Attribute
1. Self-awareness	You can identify your own emotions (Chapter 7) and know when you are acting out of your Passion or Virtue (Chapter 2).
2. Self-management	Ability to respond, not react impulsively (see CBT in Chapter 6 and NVC techniques in Chapter 9).
3. Social-Awareness	You are aware of others' needs, observe common courtesies and take others' feelings into account (Chapter 9).
4. Relationships	You cultivate healthy relationships at home, work and the community—inspiring others and yourself to work well in teams.

Each of the Instinctual Types has different barriers to raising their Emotional IQ. Self-Preservation Dominant people retreat rather than join by nature. Sexual Dominant Instinct people can find that their fending-off Instinct gets activated in a group and may have to modulate their intensity. Even the Social Dominant Instinct people have difficulties with these "playing well with others" skills if their need to lead the group creates conflicts. So we pay attention to the contribution that the Instinctual variant plays in our emotional life and apply the **Working with the Instincts** tips listed in Chapter 4.

Beyond Instinctual Type, some personality Types have a harder time with their overall emotional level and the honest display of emotions than other Types. Generally, Types 3, 7 and 8 struggle with their overall Emotional IQ, and for different reasons. Type 3s value efficiency and getting ahead in life and emotions can seem to slow them down, rendering them less capable to shine—both at work and even at home. Type 7s are so focused on gaining experiences from the outside world that they become ill-equipped to introspect and feel their full emotions. Type 8s may seem intense and full of emotional life, but much of their energy is actually from their Instinctual center, and they have trouble getting in touch with their gentler emotions. All of us needs help at times to lay down armor that prevents us from showing our emotions—showing emotional vulnerability. It's hard to open up emotionally when we never acquired the skills to do so. Type 3s benefit by saying when they don't know, they made a mistake or were caught in a social fib. Type 7s grow from getting in touch with more sadness and telling loved ones when they're down and Type 8s benefit from showing vulnerability. We can all benefit from expressing ourselves in an emotionally authentic way. If we can find one person we trust, we can explain that we are trying to express our emotions in the moment, and see our relationships take on a deeper meaning. Scary but possible.

So what can anyone with less access to emotions do? There are books on Emotional Intelligence in the **Resources** section (yes, Type 5s like to start with books first!). You might spend short periods with an emotional friend or relative and ask them questions about what makes them tick. You could try a drama or dance class where others give free expression to emotions. Art has long been a recognized therapy for the emotions. Mainly, raising your Emotional IQ means talking about your feelings in your everyday life and seeing what happens.

Meditation for Head Work

Just as we can all benefit from body and emotions work, so can we all benefit from meditation. The *Twelve Steps and Twelve Traditions* says that we XAs are active folk and that meditation can be difficult at first. It goes on to say that once we develop a prayer and meditation practice, we would "no more do without it than we would refuse air, food, or sunshine." Everyone can find more peace and build more serenity in their daily lives with meditation. There are different styles of meditation best suited for different Types.[5]

Meditation	Attribute
Mindfulness	You allow your thoughts to come; you observe them and let them go. You can also pay attention to any body sensations or feelings that arise. Bring your focus back to an object or your breath.
Focused	Involves concentration using any of the five senses—like your breath, counting mala beads, staring at a flame or listening to a gong or other sound offered on meditation apps.
Movement	This includes walking meditations in nature or in a labyrinth, yoga, qigong and 7/11 breathing (breathe in for a count of 7, and then exhale out of your mouth for a count of 11).
Mantra	Chant a mantra such as Om or search for one specific to each chakra—can be said aloud or inside your head.
Transcendental (TM)	This is a form of mantra meditation where you silently repeat your mantra whenever your mind wanders.
Spiritual	You might start with a spiritual reading and return to its idea when your mind wanders.

If you are one of the Types who need to get more connected with your Body—Types 4, 5 or 9—you could start with a movement style of meditation and conclude with one of the other forms. The Types who benefit the most from calming their minds, Types 1, 2 and 6, really thrive by starting with a spiritual reading on Serenity, Humility and Faith, respectively. People who need to express more Feelings—Types 3, 7 and 8—benefit from a mantra-based or mindfulness meditation, paying special attention to any feelings that arise and then letting them go. And we can all benefit from reading and meditating on our own Virtue or Holy Idea. If you link your Virtue to a set activity, such as eating or starting the car, you use your Virtue as a touchstone for reflection throughout your day.

Unity

Once we harmonize our Body, Heart and Head, we are on the way to our undivided self. We are playing far fewer Ego games and wasting energy to deny them to ourselves. We are changing and growing into the people we were meant to be— and for our own pleasure, not externally-motivated reasons. As Riso and Hudson said in the earlier quotation, "we simply need to discover and accept who we actually are." Don't forget the starting and ending shape for both our program of recovery and the Enneagram:

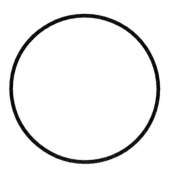

The perfect circle—is where every point is no closer or farther from the center of being than any other—it's a powerful shape, capable of containing great force. The circle of unity represents that our Ego manifestations—the Ego of our Thoughts, the Ego of our Feelings or the Ego of our Instincts—are no longer sticking out for attention. It calls for radical self-acceptance—the kind that is a byproduct of an examined life.

Very few of us will be able to totally transcend our Egos, but we can learn to live in harmony with them. We now have **Awareness** of when our mental Fixation is over-compensating, when our Heart's Passion is frustrated, and our Instinct seems threatened. We can do the work from all three centers and return to our Essence. Then we're ready to roll.

??? Questions

1. Based on the first table, what is your personal plan to do the specific work needed on your Type's center of Body, Heart or Head?

2. Add a new kind of meditation to your weekly routine, such as the three breath mini-meditation. It's been said that you may not feel the effects of meditation, but you can certainly feel when you don't do it. Does it add clarity or calmness to your life?

3. For a week, practice radical self-acceptance—just see what life brings to you. Trust that as you roll through life, you can handle the minor corrections with your HP's help, as they come up. How does this hands-off approach feel?

CHAPTER 12

OUR FORWARD-ARROW: Where Are We Headed?

STEP 12
Having had a spiritual awakening as the result of these steps, we tried to carry this message to [others] and to practice these principles in all our affairs.

I am very grateful that my Higher Power has given me a second chance to live a worthwhile life. Through Alcoholics Anonymous, I have been restored to sanity. The promises are being fulfilled in my life. I am grateful to be free from the slavery of alcohol. I am grateful for peace of mind and the opportunity to grow, but my gratitude should go forward rather than backward. I cannot stay sober on yesterday's meetings or past Twelfth-Step calls; I need to put my gratitude into action today. Our co-founder said our gratitude can best be shown by carrying the message to others. Without action, my gratitude is just a pleasant emotion. I need to put it into action by working Step Twelve, by carrying the message and practicing the principles in all my affairs. I am grateful for the chance to carry the message today![1]

—*As Bill Sees It*

I believe that the greatest truths of the universe don't lie outside, in the study of the stars and the planets. They lie deep within us, in the magnificence of our heart, mind, and soul. Until we understand what is within, we can't understand what is without.[2]

—Anita Moorjani, *Dying to Be Me*

The Past

By now we have practiced integrating our Back-Arrow's way of seeing the world. We have brought our Instincts, our emotions and our mental processes more into balance. We have a real sense of our world view opening up. Sure, there are some back-sliding days, and hopefully, we've found enough positive reinforcement from feeling our life expand that we're ready to move forward.

Moving Forward

Now it's time to move forward using our Forward-Arrow. You can find your Forward-Arrow Type in Chapter 3's **The Arrows: Your Personal Roadmap**. Reread **Passions to Virtues per Type** in Chapter 2 and **Subtype Summary** in Chapter 5 for your Forward-Arrow Type, also referred to as the "resolution point." The Forward-Arrow also offers more ways of looking at and relating to the world. The Back-Arrow contains strategies left over from childhood, but the Forward-Arrow is largely uncharted territory. You may have tried some of these traits on, but without a firm foundation of understanding your Type and Back-Arrow's Type, you likely got unsatisfactory results. Now it's time to take the momentum and added vitality from balancing your Body, Heart and Head centers to move forward.

~~~~~~

Forward-Arrow per Type

TYPE 1: Forward-Arrow Type 4 Envy → Equanimity

Type 1s picked up some needed flexibility and fun of Sobriety from their Back-Arrow Type 7. Now you can practice Awareness of the low side of Type 4's Envy. Perfectionism gets tiring. Maybe you've already begun to look at other people having far more fun without so many self-imposed rules. This looking outside oneself in comparison is Envy. The relief from such comparisons that only compound Type 1's judgment is to reach for Equanimity. Equanimity is humble because it sees us all as equal. My needs are no more important to me than yours are to you. Equanimity requires trust—trust that we can't win our HP's favor by being "good"—that we all live in grace.

Forward-Arrow Work: Try seeing others' right to live as they choose as freeing for you. You don't need to waste any more energy inspecting how others are managing. The bumper sticker "Live & Let Live" has two great parts—and by your making your own life as full and fulfilling as you can, you'll be too busy to worry about others. You can come back to your home Type's Virtue of knowing who you are and where you stand with Sobriety, Serenity and Equanimity.

TYPE 2: Forward-Arrow Type 8 Lust → Innocence
Type 2s went back to reclaim emotional authenticity by reintegrating Equanimity from their Back-Arrow Type 4. Now you may be shocked at some bossy take-charge-ness coming from Type 8 Lust. Good—that nice act wasn't showing the world all of who you are. Lust is spotting what you want and *going* for it. Show yourself lots of self-compassion because it's harder in many ways for overly mannerly people to toughen up than for tough people to relax some. Innocence, that wonderful unguarded quality, is just around the corner.

Forward-Arrow Work: Both of your arrows point you toward stepping firmly into the middle of your own life and owning your power. Type 8s are the powerhouses, and you have some of that in you. Ask clearly for what you'd like—you may not get it, but you will have been clear. Grant yourself the right to say No, too. Your bumper sticker, "Humility is not thinking less of yourself, but thinking of yourself less" means there's no need to play small anymore. When you mix your Virtue of Humility with Type 4's Equanimity and finally add Innocence, you'll step into the large life you were meant to have with your HP.

TYPE 3: Forward-Arrow Type 9   Sloth → Right Action

Type 3s have faced the anxiety that was under the surface and learned to match Fear with Courage from integrating their Back-Arrow Type 6. You might be getting in touch with the Fear that was propelling you into too much action. Sloth can be your pause button as you figure out your true values and get inspired with the Right Action to move toward "a new freedom and a new happiness."[3] Right Action is not you reverting to your home Type's strategy of managing well—it's pausing and waiting for the intuitive thought to choose what's best for the real you.

Forward-Arrow Work: Good advice in early recovery was to pause and ask, "Is this action likely to take me closer to a slip or closer to recovery?" That same decision tree will help you now if you ask yourself, "Will this action bring me closer to my vibrant, authentic self?" Your bumper sticker, from a profound statement in Hamlet, says "To thine own self be true . . . Thou canst not then be false to any man" means that knowing yourself creates a strength that comes from the inside-out. Your trio of past-present and future Virtues of Courage, Veracity and Right Action will allow you to grow into your strong and emotionally real self.

TYPE 4: Forward-Arrow Type 2 Pride → Humility

Type 4s came to know themselves more clearly through reaching back for Type 1's Serenity. Now it's time to try on Type 2's Pride and Humility. You needed to get grounded first but now are able to take on some of the Helper's role in service. Type 2 offers a path of extroversion—away from the bondage of self that Type 4s experience and into more sunlight with others. At first, you may feel the swell of Pride in helping others. That's fine because Type 4s already understand that much of what we do is for ourselves too. Humility is not taking too much credit for the good you bring. As the Saint Francis prayer says in *Twelve Steps and Twelve Traditions*, "Make me a *channel* of thy peace"[4]—just the channel.

Forward-Arrow Work: Your home Type Virtue of Equanimity goes well with this new Virtue of Humility. Both require an accurate assessment to find someplace in the middle. For the SO4s, this will mean bringing up self-esteem—no more playing less-than for others to see you. For the SX4s, Humility means thinking of yourself less, and for the SP4s, it requires Humility to ask for help. Your personal bumper sticker is "Attitude of Gratitude" and includes gratitude for all that's lovely inside as well. With Serenity to accept your Equanimity, you can go forth with Humility to share your talents.

TYPE 5: Forward-Arrow Type 7 Gluttony → Sobriety

Type 5s needed to get more proactive in stating their needs using Type 8's Innocence and confidence in the world. Going forward can be scary for Type 5s because they see their old vice of Gluttony. Gluttony is addictively filling the spiritual hole with things that can't satisfy. Type 5s made up a strategy of not asking for much and not giving extra, and here's this whole tide of abundance threatening to wash over them. But once you let the floodgates down, you *are* likely to get overwhelmed by life's choices. Ride out the rapids for a while because there's the calm of Sobriety ahead. Sobriety is more calmly choosing from the great abundance life offers. Sobriety is knowing that even without your well thought out plans, all will be all right.

Forward-Arrow Work: What Type 7 opens up for you is a lot more spontaneity and playfulness—a needed balance for your seriousness. Rather than look toward the future with fear and trepidation, Type 7 challenges you to look forward with excitement for all the unknown possibilities. Your bumper sticker is "Oh, Lighten Up!" and you know why. If you can start each day without the carryover from past hurts in Innocence, you can live in Nonattachment to let both good and bad come and go—you can savor the abundance of life in Sobriety.

TYPE 6: Forward-Arrow Type 3   Deceit → Veracity

Type 6s got more grounded in the here and now adopting Type 9's Instinctual Right Action. Now it's time to have Courage—to doubt less and step into your true self with Veracity. What Type 3 offers is "pulling it together" to get a job done with charm and confidence. Type 3's Deceit presents an image of how they would like to be seen that seems opposite to your Type's demand for trustworthiness. Once you practice Acceptance of how we all want to be seen in a favorable light, you can work toward Veracity and become your more effective real self.

Forward-Arrow Work: Rather than get stuck in Fear, you can benefit from Type 3's confidence to "keep your eyes on the prize" to accomplish your goal and then stay and take credit for it. Go into action after shorter analysis, and don't be afraid to stand out more. Remember: "Face Everything And Recover." When you take Right Action with Courage, you need not run from fears, both internal and external and can settle into your own Veracity.

TYPE 7: Forward-Arrow Type 1   Anger → Serenity

Type 7s have slowed their grab for **MORE** using Nonattachment from Type 5. You may be wondering where your lighthearted optimism went as you go forward toward Type 1's Serenity. You may shock yourself when you observe real Anger under your funny cajoling ways to get people to do things your way. Real Anger was there all along, so you might as well make friends with it and let it inform you when your needs are not met, or your demands are too great.

Forward-Arrow Work: Accepting structure and time commitments is difficult, but in this maturing process called life, you'll gain Serenity when you do. Type 1 attributes will help you focus your many talents to accomplish what others expect—and gain more time to do what you want to do. "We do not tire so easily, for we are not burning up energy foolishly," as it says in the Big Book.[5] Your bumper sticker is "A Day at a Time" as a reminder to stop living in the future and enjoy *now*. It seems you gain the biggest prizes of all. When you are Nonattached to getting your way, you have the Sobriety to stop and savor what you have—and that's Serenity.

TYPE 8: Forward-Arrow Type 5   Greed → Nonattachment

Type 8's obsession to exert power over their environment has been moderated by getting in touch with Humility by asking for their own needs with Innocence. Going forward means adding Type 5's Nonattachment to "do the action and turn over the results." Your bumper sticker is "Easy Does It!" as a reminder to turn over those results. When first integrating this new Type, you may observe your Greed to protect what you've won. Hopefully, you see how the truly strong can be more open, which includes being open to sadness when the good things leave, or when we can't get what we want.

Forward-Arrow Work: Adding Type 5 to your toolbox is turning down the volume from your Instinctual Body center and giving way to Thoughts and Feelings more. This growth entails deeper introspection to explore where your feelings come from and slowing down to observe your mind's processes. With Humility and Innocence, you can accept all that life offers and welcome Nonattachment to let it go too.

TYPE 9: Forward-Arrow Type 6   Fear → Courage

Type 9s gained some bravado from Type 3s until the "fake it 'til you make it" became Veracity. Now it's time to face the Fear that can paralyze you back into Sloth. What Type 6 offers Type 9 is more solidness—it helps bring your idealism back to earth. Their traits can wake you up to what you *should* worry about. Fear of giving up responsibility and living a half-life can push you toward Courage. You can choose to act, and you can choose to be exactly you.

Forward-Arrow Work: Borrow some of Type 6's quality of outspokenness when you are next tempted to keep the peace at any price to yourself. You can take a stand when you realize your opinion will also help "our common welfare." Your bumper sticker reads "First Things First" because it requires Veracity of knowing who you are to take Right Action and then take more of a stand in life—in Courage.

~~~~~~

Your Type's Slogan

Type	Your Bumper Sticker
1	Live & Let Live
2	Humility is not thinking less of yourself, but thinking of yourself less
3	To Thine Own Self Be True
4	Attitude of Gratitude
5	Oh, Lighten Up! (not Think Think Think)
6	Face Everything And Recover
7	A Day at a Time
8	Easy Does It!
9	First Things First

Recap of All Your Work

Remember "What an order! I can't go through with it" when the whole Enneagram path was laid out in Chapter 2? The Enneagram's practical spirituality aligns so well with what we're trying to accomplish in recovery. We sensed that our Ego was at the root of ongoing problems but needed a new perspective to chart where we're headed and how to get there. We have used the same coping strategy so habitually for so long that those pathways may seem etched in stone. The good news that scientists have found regarding our brains is that our neural networks actually display neural plasticity—and so can the totality of us change.

We may have needed the armor of our Body-Heart-Head Egos in the form of our Instincts-Passions and Fixations. But as spiritual beings who have undergone growth through **Awareness-Acceptance-Action**, that armor is restrictive now and we're beginning to shed much of it. We're peeling the layers of the onion back to our Essence.

It could appear that we've been splitting the human being into Head-Body-Heart, but that was only to work on one area at a time. We know that we are holistic beings and are indivisible in our Essence. The Enneagram shows us how to deconstruct the Ego that would like to keep us safe and stuck and trade it in for a bigger life.

??? Questions

1. If you're not quite ready to integrate your Forward-Arrow Type, could you get to know some people from that Type to see the benefits?

2. Practice the suggestions for your Forward-Arrow Subtype from Chapter 5. Considering that your Forward-Arrow Type needs some of what you have, are you already practicing some of these traits?

3. Practice and record examples of work for your Forward-Arrow Type.

Congratulations!

What an order—and you *did* go through with it. Really feeling how our Type is limiting us will take a lifetime. Your Back-Arrow Type will integrate into your own Type because of the urge left from childhood but the Forward-Arrow work will likely take much longer.

Here is your personal **Ongoing Spiritual Growth Plan** to keep track of your progress and which aspects need work. Happy trudging . . .

Ongoing Spiritual Growth Plan

TYPE 1: "Perfectionist"

_____ You can spot the Passion and live in the Virtue of your Back-Arrow Type more than half the time: Type 7 **Gluttony → Sobriety**

_____ You can spot the Fixation and live in the Holy Idea of your Back-Arrow Type more than half the time: Type 7 **Planning → Holy Plan**

_____ You can spot the Passion and live in the Virtue of your home Type more than half the time: Type 1 **Anger → Serenity**

_____ You can spot the Fixation and live in the Holy Idea of your home Type more than half the time: Type 1 **Resentment → Holy Perfection**

_____ You have taken 10% of your energy away from your Dominant Instinct and given that time and energy to your Repressed Instinct

_____ You have started to balance your emotions by expressing more of the emotions that were low before: Fear, Anger, Sadness, Joy

_____ You can catch yourself in Ego when competing with someone similar for the same Ego turf

_____ You look for similarities between you and dissimilar people who bother you and acknowledge your common need

_____ You express your needs and feelings using "I statements" using NVC or another technique to communicate better

_____ You can spot the Passion and live in the Virtue of your Wing Type much of the time: Type 9 **Sloth → Right Action**

_____ You can spot the Passion and live in the Virtue of your Wing Type much of the time: Type 2 **Pride → Humility**

_____ You are bringing up the centers that are low for you through Body Work; managing Emotional Reactivity and finding new forms of meditation for your Mental center

_____ You can spot the Passion and live in the Virtue of your Forward-Arrow Type much of the time: Type 4 **Envy → Equanimity**

_____ You can spot the Fixation and live in the Holy Idea of your Forward-Arrow Type much of the time: Type 4 **Melancholy → Holy Origin**

Ongoing Spiritual Growth Plan

TYPE 2: "Helper"

_____ You can spot the Passion and live in the Virtue of your Back-Arrow Type more than half the time: Type 4 **Envy →
Equanimity**

_____ You can spot the Fixation and live in the Holy Idea of your Back-Arrow Type more than half the time: Type 4
Melancholy → Holy Origin

_____ You can spot the Passion and live in the Virtue of your home Type more than half the time: Type 2 **Pride → Humility**

_____ You can spot the Fixation and live in the Holy Idea of your home Type more than half the time: Type 2 **Flattery →
Holy Will**

_____ You have taken 10% of your energy away from your Dominant Instinct and given that time and energy to your Repressed Instinct

_____ You have started to balance your emotions by expressing more of the emotions that were low before: Fear, Anger, Sadness, Joy

_____ You can catch yourself in Ego when competing with someone similar for the same Ego turf

_____ You look for similarities between you and dissimilar people who bother you and acknowledge your common need

_____ You express your needs and feelings using "I statements" using NVC or another technique to communicate better

_____ You can spot the Passion and live in the Virtue of your Wing Type much of the time: Type 1 **Anger → Serenity**

_____ You can spot the Passion and live in the Virtue of your Wing Type much of the time: Type 3 **Deceit → Veracity**

_____ You are bringing up the centers that are low for you through Body Work; managing Emotional Reactivity and finding new forms of meditation for your Mental center

_____ You can spot the Passion and live in the Virtue of your Forward-Arrow Type much of the time: Type 8 **Lust →
Innocence**

_____ You can spot the Fixation and live in the Holy Idea of your Forward-Arrow Type much of the time: Type 8 **Revenge →
Holy Truth**

Ongoing Spiritual Growth Plan

TYPE 3: "Achiever"

_____ You can spot the Passion and live in the Virtue of your Back-Arrow Type more than half the time: Type 6 **Fear →
Courage**

_____ You can spot the Fixation and live in the Holy Idea of your Back-Arrow Type more than half the time: Type 6
Cowardice → Holy Faith

_____ You can spot the Passion and live in the Virtue of your home Type more than half the time: Type 3 **Deceit → Veracity**

_____ You can spot the Fixation and live in the Holy Idea of your home Type more than half the time: Type 3 **Vanity → Holy Law**

_____ You have taken 10% of your energy away from your Dominant Instinct and given that time and energy to your Repressed Instinct

_____ You have started to balance your emotions by expressing more of the emotions that were low before: Fear, Anger, Sadness, Joy

_____ You can catch yourself in Ego when competing with someone similar for the same Ego turf

_____ You look for similarities between you and dissimilar people who bother you and acknowledge your common need

_____ You express your needs and feelings using "I statements" using NVC or another technique to communicate better

_____ You can spot the Passion and live in the Virtue of your Wing Type much of the time: Type 2 **Pride → Humility**

_____ You can spot the Passion and live in the Virtue of your Wing Type much of the time: Type 4 **Envy → Equanimity**

_____ You are bringing up the centers that are low for you through Body Work; managing Emotional Reactivity and finding new forms of meditation for your Mental center

_____ You can spot the Passion and live in the Virtue of your Forward-Arrow Type much of the time: Type 9 **Sloth →
Right Action**

_____ You can spot the Fixation and live in the Holy Idea of your Forward-Arrow Type much of the time: Type 9 **Indolence
→ Holy Love**

Ongoing Spiritual Growth Plan

TYPE 4: "Individualist"

_____ You can spot the Passion and live in the Virtue of your Back-Arrow Type more than half the time: Type 1 **Anger → Serenity**

_____ You can spot the Fixation and live in the Holy Idea of your Back-Arrow Type more than half the time: Type 1 **Resentment → Holy Perfection**

_____ You can spot the Passion and live in the Virtue of your home Type more than half the time: Type 4 **Envy → Equanimity**

_____ You can spot the Fixation and live in the Holy Idea of your home Type more than half the time: Type 4 **Melancholy → Holy Origin**

_____ You have taken 10% of your energy away from your Dominant Instinct and given that time and energy to your Repressed Instinct

_____ You have started to balance your emotions by expressing more of the emotions that were low before: Fear, Anger, Sadness, Joy

_____ You can catch yourself in Ego when competing with someone similar for the same Ego turf

_____ You look for similarities between you and dissimilar people who bother you and acknowledge your common need

_____ You express your needs and feelings using "I statements" using NVC or another technique to communicate better

_____ You can spot the Passion and live in the Virtue of your Wing Type much of the time: Type 3 **Deceit → Veracity**

_____ You can spot the Passion and live in the Virtue of your Wing Type much of the time: Type 5 **Greed/Avarice → Nonattachment**

_____ You are bringing up the centers that are low for you through Body Work; managing Emotional Reactivity and finding new forms of meditation for your Mental center

_____ You can spot the Passion and live in the Virtue of your Forward-Arrow Type much of the time: Type 2 **Pride → Humility**

_____ You can spot the Fixation and live in the Holy Idea of your Forward-Arrow Type much of the time: Type 2 **Flattery → Holy Will**

Ongoing Spiritual Growth Plan

TYPE 5: "Observer"

_____ You can spot the Passion and live in the Virtue of your Back-Arrow Type more than half the time: Type 8 **Lust →
Innocence**

_____ You can spot the Fixation and live in the Holy Idea of your Back-Arrow Type more than half the time: Type 8 **Revenge
→ Holy Truth**

_____ You can spot the Passion and live in the Virtue of your home Type more than half the time: Type 5 **Greed/Avarice →
Nonattachment**

_____ You can spot the Fixation and live in the Holy Idea of your home Type more than half the time: Type 5 **Stinginess →
Holy Omniscience**

_____ You have taken 10% of your energy away from your Dominant Instinct and given that time and energy to your Repressed Instinct

_____ You have started to balance your emotions by expressing more of the emotions that were low before: Fear, Anger, Sadness, Joy

_____ You can catch yourself in Ego when competing with someone similar for the same Ego turf

_____ You look for similarities between you and dissimilar people who bother you and acknowledge your common need

_____ You express your needs and feelings using "I statements" using NVC or another technique to communicate better

_____ You can spot the Passion and live in the Virtue of your Wing Type much of the time: Type 4 **Envy → Equanimity**

_____ You can spot the Passion and live in the Virtue of your Wing Type much of the time: Type 6 **Fear → Courage**

_____ You are bringing up the centers that are low for you through Body Work; managing Emotional Reactivity and finding new forms of meditation for your Mental center

_____ You can spot the Passion and live in the Virtue of your Forward-Arrow Type much of the time: Type 7 **Gluttony →
Sobriety**

_____ You can spot the Fixation and live in the Holy Idea of your Forward-Arrow Type much of the time: Type 7 **Planning →
Holy Plan**

Ongoing Spiritual Growth Plan

TYPE 6: "Loyalist"

_____ You can spot the Passion and live in the Virtue of your Back-Arrow Type more than half the time: Type 9 **Sloth → Right Action**

_____ You can spot the Fixation and live in the Holy Idea of your Back-Arrow Type more than half the time: Type 9 **Indolence → Holy Love**

_____ You can spot the Passion and live in the Virtue of your home Type more than half the time: Type 6 **Fear → Courage**

_____ You can spot the Fixation and live in the Holy Idea of your home Type more than half the time: Type 6 **Cowardice → Holy Faith**

_____ You have taken 10% of your energy away from your Dominant Instinct and given that time and energy to your Repressed Instinct

_____ You have started to balance your emotions by expressing more of the emotions that were low before: Fear, Anger, Sadness, Joy

_____ You can catch yourself in Ego when competing with someone similar for the same Ego turf

_____ You look for similarities between you and dissimilar people who bother you and acknowledge your common need

_____ You express your needs and feelings using "I statements" using NVC or another technique to communicate better

_____ You can spot the Passion and live in the Virtue of your Wing Type much of the time: Type 5 **Greed/Avarice → Nonattachment**

_____ You can spot the Passion and live in the Virtue of your Wing Type much of the time: Type 7 **Gluttony → Sobriety**

_____ You are bringing up the centers that are low for you through Body Work; managing Emotional Reactivity and finding new forms of meditation for your Mental center

_____ You can spot the Passion and live in the Virtue of your Forward-Arrow Type much of the time: Type 3 **Deceit → Veracity**

_____ You can spot the Fixation and live in the Holy Idea of your Forward-Arrow Type much of the time: Type 3 **Vanity → Holy Law**

Ongoing Spiritual Growth Plan

TYPE 7: "Adventurer"

_____ You can spot the Passion and live in the Virtue of your Back-Arrow Type more than half the time: Type 5
     Greed/Avarice → Nonattachment

_____ You can spot the Fixation and live in the Holy Idea of your Back-Arrow Type more than half the time: Type 5
     Stinginess → Holy Omniscience

_____ You can spot the Passion and live in the Virtue of your home Type more than half the time: Type 7 **Planning → Holy Plan**

_____ You can spot the Fixation and live in the Holy Idea of your home Type more than half the time: Type 7 **Planning → Holy Plan**

_____ You have taken 10% of your energy away from your Dominant Instinct and given that time and energy to your Repressed Instinct

_____ You have started to balance your emotions by expressing more of the emotions that were low before: Fear, Anger, Sadness, Joy

_____ You can catch yourself in Ego when competing with someone similar for the same Ego turf

_____ You look for similarities between you and dissimilar people who bother you and acknowledge your common need

_____ You express your needs and feelings using "I statements" using NVC or another technique to communicate better

_____ You can spot the Passion and live in the Virtue of your Wing Type much of the time: Type 6 **Fear → Courage**

_____ You can spot the Passion and live in the Virtue of your Wing Type much of the time: Type 8 **Lust → Innocence**

_____ You are bringing up the centers that are low for you through Body Work; managing Emotional Reactivity and finding new forms of meditation for your Mental center

_____ You can spot the Passion and live in the Virtue of your Forward-Arrow Type much of the time: Type 1 **Anger → Serenity**

_____ You can spot the Fixation and live in the Holy Idea of your Forward-Arrow Type much of the time: Type 1
     Resentment → Holy Perfection

Ongoing Spiritual Growth Plan

TYPE 8: "Leader"

_____ You can spot the Passion and live in the Virtue of your Back-Arrow Type more than half the time: Type 2 **Pride → Humility**

_____ You can spot the Fixation and live in the Holy Idea of your Back-Arrow Type more than half the time: Type 2 **Flattery → Holy Will**

_____ You can spot the Passion and live in the Virtue of your home Type more than half the time: Type 8 **Lust → Innocence**

_____ You can spot the Fixation and live in the Holy Idea of your home Type more than half the time: Type 8 **Revenge → Holy Truth**

_____ You have taken 10% of your energy away from your Dominant Instinct and given that time and energy to your Repressed Instinct

_____ You have started to balance your emotions by expressing more of the emotions that were low before: Fear, Anger, Sadness, Joy

_____ You can catch yourself in Ego when competing with someone similar for the same Ego turf

_____ You look for similarities between you and dissimilar people who bother you and acknowledge your common need

_____ You express your needs and feelings using "I statements" using NVC or another technique to communicate better

_____ You can spot the Passion and live in the Virtue of your Wing Type much of the time: Type 7 **Gluttony → Sobriety**

_____ You can spot the Passion and live in the Virtue of your Wing Type much of the time: Type 9 **Sloth → Right Action**

_____ You are bringing up the centers that are low for you through Body Work; managing Emotional Reactivity and finding new forms of meditation for your Mental center

_____ You can spot the Passion and live in the Virtue of your Forward-Arrow Type much of the time: Type 5 **Greed/Avarice → Nonattachment**

_____ You can spot the Fixation and live in the Holy Idea of your Forward-Arrow Type much of the time: Type 5 **Stinginess → Holy Omniscience**

Ongoing Spiritual Growth Plan

TYPE 9: "Peacemaker"

_____ You can spot the Passion and live in the Virtue of your Back-Arrow Type more than half the time: Type 3 **Deceit → Veracity**

_____ You can spot the Fixation and live in the Holy Idea of your Back-Arrow Type more than half the time: Type 3 **Vanity → Holy Law**

_____ You can spot the Passion and live in the Virtue of your home Type more than half the time: Type 9 **Sloth → Right Action**

_____ You can spot the Fixation and live in the Holy Idea of your home Type more than half the time: Type 9 **Indolence → Holy Love**

_____ You have taken 10% of your energy away from your Dominant Instinct and given that time and energy to your Repressed Instinct

_____ You have started to balance your emotions by expressing more of the emotions that were low before: Fear, Anger, Sadness, Joy

_____ You can catch yourself in Ego when competing with someone similar for the same Ego turf

_____ You look for similarities between you and dissimilar people who bother you and acknowledge your common need

_____ You express your needs and feelings using "I statements" using NVC or another technique to communicate better

_____ You can spot the Passion and live in the Virtue of your Wing Type much of the time: Type 8 **Lust → Innocence**

_____ You can spot the Passion and live in the Virtue of your Wing Type much of the time: Type 1 **Anger → Serenity**

_____ You are bringing up the centers that are low for you through Body Work; managing Emotional Reactivity and finding new forms of meditation for your Mental center

_____ You can spot the Passion and live in the Virtue of your Forward-Arrow Type much of the time: Type 6 **Fear → Courage**

_____ You can spot the Fixation and live in the Holy Idea of your Forward-Arrow Type much of the time: Type 6 **Cowardice → Holy Faith**

Parting Thoughts

We have used **Awareness—Acceptance—Action** to shine light on previously unseen defects and assets. As it says in the Big Book, "That being so you have swallowed and digested some big chunks of truth about yourself."[6] Using the Enneagram speeds up our spiritual growth by highlighting our particular traps and the best way toward our Virtues and Holy Ideas. The Enneagram points to what we needed to face from childhood in our Back-Arrow Type, how to get the balance from our Wing Types and finally points us toward the Virtues that could be ours in our Forward-Arrow Type.

I hope this path calls to you. Even if you're doubtful that one of your Arrow Types is good for you, try it on for a while—really "act as if"—and see what happens. The plan of action described here has an ambitious timeline. Any one of the activities could be practiced for months before progressing. You may choose to work at a slower and deeper level or try this once-over-quickly pace to peel the onion. The Twelve Steps are often repeated as we are able to see more about ourselves, and so can the Enneagram process be repeated. And this "trying it on" for a while is a good trick not to scare our Egos who'd like to stay in charge. We can always go back to how we were, at least for a while.

That's why finding an Enneagram group and/or coach can be vital. Like in our recovery program, we're apt to give up if we're not reminded that our commitment to psychological-spiritual work is important and doable. People sharing in an Enneagram group speak of their struggles, and it's helpful to be reminded that what we're trying is hard, requires persistence and a lot of self-compassion. People in recovery know that a one-time spiritual experience can recede to nothing unless followed by ever-deepening work. So search for an Enneagram group in your area or create one with friends in recovery to share in this new journey.

One last wish: we have accepted that we will probably adopt new traits awkwardly—so explain this to the people near to you and let yourself be messy psychologically. But try not to add new behavior to buttress up the old Ego. As my teacher told me when I complained of new bursts of anger— "Anger for you is fine if you are using it to fight for a real relationship *toward* people, but it's not alright if you are using it to keep them away, as Type 5s like to do." So, my friends of every Type, move forward in Love and not in Fear, and all will be well.

MY GRATITUDES

I am grateful for a loving Higher Power.
I am grateful for my daughter who gave me someone to love.
I am grateful for my Fellowship that saved my life and gave me a life of meaning.
I am grateful for this beautiful planet and a strong body to explore it.
I am grateful for friends, sponsors and sponsees in the Fellowship.
I am grateful for teachers, friends and mentors in the Enneagram community.
I am grateful for my teachers Dr Beatrice Chestnut, Uranio Paes and Nancy Hunterton.
I am grateful for a (mostly) sound mind.
I am grateful for *all* of my emotions.
I am grateful for all of you reading this who have formed an unseen community.

NOTES

INTRODUCTION
1. *Alcoholics Anonymous*, 4th ed. (New York: Alcoholics Anonymous World Services, Inc., 2001), 328.
2. Jeff Myers. "P.D. Ouspensky." *Gurdjieff Work*, 2012, www.gurdjieffwork.com/site/index.asp?page=110280&DL =243. Accessed 8 June 2020.
3. *Alcoholics Anonymous*, 130.

CHAPTER 1
1. *Twelve Steps and Twelve Traditions* (New York: Alcoholics Anonymous World Services, Inc., 1952), 46.
2. Richard Rohr. *Breathing Under Water: Spirituality and the Twelve Steps* (Cincinnati: St. Anthony Messenger Press, 2011), xviii.
3. Claudio Naranjo. *The Enneagram of Society: Healing the Soul to Heal the World.* Translated by Paul Barnes (Nevada City: Gateway Books and Tapes, 2004), 25.
4. Oscar Ichazo. *Interviews with Oscar Ichazo* (New York: Arica Institute Press, 1982), 13.
5. Michael Powers, "Emotional Sobriety." *EmotSob2*, 29 March 2018, www.michaelppowers.com/path/emotsob2.html, Accessed 20 September 2020.
6. Nathaniel Branden. *The Disowned Self* (New York: Bantam, 1984), 99.
7. Dean C. "What are the Principles?" *The e-AA Group*, 2000, www.e-aa.org/forum/viewtopic.php?f=12&t=845. Accessed 27 July 2020.
8. *Alcoholics Anonymous*, 45.
9. *Alcoholics Anonymous*, 84.

CHAPTER 2
1. *Alcoholics Anonymous*, 85.
2. Kathleen Hurley and Theodore Dobson. *My Best Self: Using the Enneagram to Free the Soul* (New York: HarperCollins Publishers, 1993), 92.

3. *Alcoholics Anonymous*, 60.
4. *Twelve Steps and Twelve Traditions*, 66.

CHAPTER 3
1. *Alcoholics Anonymous*, 62.
2. Beatrice Chestnut. *The Complete Enneagram: 27 Paths to Greater Self-Knowledge* (Berkeley: She Writes Press, 2013), 42.
3. *Alcoholics Anonymous*, 82.
4. *Alcoholics Anonymous*, 528.

CHAPTER 4
1. *Twelve Steps and Twelve Traditions*, 42.
2. Sandra Maitri. *The Enneagram of Passions and Virtues: Finding the Way Home* (New York: Penguin Group, 2005), 12.
3. Oosterwijk, S., Lindquist, K. A., Anderson, E., Dautoff, R., Moriguchi, Y., & Barrett, L. F. (2012). States of mind: emotions, body feelings, and thoughts share distributed neural networks. *NeuroImage, 62*(3), 2110–2128. doi.org/10.1016/j.neuroimage.2012.05.079
4. Eric Salmon. *Subtypes: The Key to the Enneagram.* Translated by Heather Brown (Leaping Boy Publications, 2016), 41.
5. *Alcoholics Anonymous*, 62.
6. *Alcoholics Anonymous*, 87.

CHAPTER 5
1. *Alcoholics Anonymous*, 55.
2. *The Complete Enneagram*, 26.
3. *Alcoholics Anonymous*, 67.
4. *Twelve Steps and Twelve Traditions*, 57.
5. *Alcoholics Anonymous*, 133.
6. *Twelve Steps and Twelve Traditions*, 53.
7. *Alcoholics Anonymous*, 87.
8. *Twelve Steps and Twelve Traditions*, 60.

CHAPTER 6

1. *Alcoholics Anonymous,* 23.
2. Uranio Paes, "Understanding the Enneagram Fixations." *Mundoeneagrama*, 29 November 2016, www.mundoeneagrama.com/learning-community /videos/post/understanding-the-enneagram-fixations. Accessed 8 August 2020.
3. Hofmann SG, Asnaani A, Vonk IJ, Sawyer AT, Fang A. The efficacy of cognitive behavioral therapy: A review of meta-analyses. *Cognit Ther Res.* 2012;36(5):427-440. doi:10.1007/s10608-012-9476-1
4. Mathew McKay, Martha Davis and Patrick Fanning. *Thoughts & Feelings: Taking Control of Your Moods and Your Life* (Oakland: New Harbinger Publications, Inc., 1997), 32-40.

CHAPTER 7

1. *Alcoholics Anonymous,* 133.
2. Fred H. *Drop the Rock—The Ripple Effect* (Center City: Hazelden Publishing, 2016), 26-27.
3. Bill W. *Emotional Sobriety II—The Next Frontier* (New York: AAGrapevine, Inc., 2011), IX.
4. *Drop the Rock*, 28.
5. *Twelve Steps and Twelve Traditions*, 149.
6. Joseph P. Forgas. "Four Ways Sadness May Be Good for You." *Greater Good*, 4 June 2014, greatergood.berkeley.edu/article/item/four_ways_sadness _may_be_good_for_you. Accessed 28 July 2020.
7. Leonard Cohen. "Anthem." *The Future*, Legacy, 5 January 2008. www.azlyrics.com/lyrics/leonardcohen/anthem.html, Accessed 13 August 2020.
8. *The Disowned Self*, 99.
9. Don Richard Riso with Russ Hudson. *Personality Types* (Boston: Houghton Mifflin, 1987, 1996), 29

CHAPTER 8

1. *Alcoholics Anonymous,* 73.
2. Carl Jung. *Collected Works Vol. 11 Psychology and Religion: West and East* (London: Routledge and Kegan Paul, 1973), 131.
3. *Twelve Steps and Twelve Traditions,* 27.
4. MediaWiki. "Shadow (psychology)." *Wikipedia,* 2020, en.wikipedia.org/wiki/Shadow_(psychology). Accessed 26 July 2020.
5. *Twelve Steps and Twelve Traditions,* 77.
6. *Alcoholics Anonymous,* 552.
7. *Twelve Steps and Twelve Traditions,* 49.
8. Destiny Lopez, Natalie Baker and Kerry Nenn. "Gestalt Therapy: The Empty Chair Technique." *MentalHelp.net,* 2020, www.mentalhelp.net/blogs/gestalt-therapy-the-empty-chair-technique/. Accessed 13 August 2020.

CHAPTER 9

1. "Madtv-Bob Newhart Skit-Mo Collins-Stop it" *YouTube,* 2010, www.youtube.com/watch?v=HiELt6VhSaQ. Accessed 8 August 2020.
2. *Twelve Steps and Twelve Traditions,* 52.
3. Marshall Rosenberg. *Nonviolent Communication,* 3rd ed. (Encinitas: PuddleDancer Press, 2015), 31.
4. *Alcoholics Anonymous,* 550-551.
5. *Twelve Steps and Twelve Traditions,* 80.
6. Ken Wilber. "Taking Responsibility for Your Shadow." *Meeting the Shadow,* edited by Connie Zweig and Jeremiah Abrams (New York: Penguin, 1991), 274.
7. *Twelve Steps and Twelve Traditions,* 90.
8. *Twelve Steps and Twelve Traditions,* 77.
9. *Nonviolent Communication,* 30-255.
10. Marshall Rosenberg, "Needs Inventory." *The Center for Nonviolent Communication,* 2005, www.cnvc.org/training/resource/needs-inventory. Accessed 27 June 2020.

11. Marshall Rosenberg, "Feelings Inventory." *The Center for Nonviolent Communication*, 2005, www.cnvc.org/training/resource/feelings-inventory. Accessed 27 June 2020.

CHAPTER 10
1. *Twelve Steps and Twelve Traditions*, 89.
2. *Personality Types*, 43.
3. *Personality Types*, 90-408.

CHAPTER 11
1. *Twelve Steps and Twelve Traditions*, 97.
2. Don Richard Riso and Russ Hudson. *The Wisdom of the Enneagram* (New York: Bantam Books, 1999), 41.
3. *Personality Types*, 29.
4. Mihaly Csikszentmihalyi. *Flow: The Psychology of Optimal Experience* (New York: Harper Collins, 1990), 39.
5. Holly J. Bertone, reviewed by Janna Young. "Which Type of Meditation is Right for Me?" *Healthline*, 9 June 2017, www.healthline.com/health/mental-health/types-of-meditation#mindfulness-meditation. Accessed 12 July 2020.

CHAPTER 12
1. *As Bill Sees It* (New York: Alcoholics Anonymous World Services, Inc., 2001), 29.
2. Anita Moorjani. *Dying to Be Me: My Journey from Cancer, to Near Death, to True Healing* (Carlsbad: Hay House, 2012), 110.
3. *Alcoholics Anonymous*, 84.
4. *Twelve Steps and Twelve Traditions*, 99.
5. *Alcoholics Anonymous*, 88.
6. *Alcoholics Anonymous*, 71.

RESOURCES

Online

Enneagram quizzes:
    Free EclecticEnergies
    www.eclecticenergies.com/enneagram/test-2
    Commercial iEQ9 www.integrative9.com/getyourtype/?
        gclid=EAIaIQobChMI47KxrtfV6wIV9T6tBh2j5wVDEA
        AYASABEgJAvPD_BwE
    RHETI www.enneagraminstitute.com/rheti
Certified Enneagram coaches Certified Coaches
    cpenneagram.com/front-page/certified-professionals/
In-depth videos on all aspects of the Enneagram: Chestnut
    Paes Enneagram Online www.mundoeneagrama.com/
    and
Subtype explanation: CPEA
    cpenneagram.com/category/enneagram-2-0-podcast/
Beautifully written blogs on the Enneagram and the 12 Steps:
    nakedheartrecovery.org/
Marshall Rosenberg, Nonviolent Communication
    video: www.youtube.com/watch?v=UEqmZ2E1o64
    Download Needs Inventory
        www.cnvc.org/training/resource/needs-inventory
    Download Feelings Inventory
        www.cnvc.org/training/resource/feelings-inventory
    (c) 2005 by Center for Nonviolent Communication
    Website: www.cnvc.org Email: cnvc@cnvc.org Phone:
    +1.505-244-4041

Books

Beatrice Chestnut, *The Complete Enneagram: 27 Paths to
    Greater Self-Knowledge*
Sandra Maitri, *The Enneagram of Passions and Virtues*
Richard Rohr, *Breathing Under Water: Spirituality and the
    Twelve Steps*
Richard Rohr, *Enneagram II*
Don Richard Riso and Russ Hudson, *The Wisdom of the
    Enneagram*

Emotional IQ books
  Brandon Goleman, *Emotional Intelligence*
  Justin Bariso, *EQ Applied: The Real-World Guide to Emotional Intelligence*
Cognitive Behavior Therapy (CBT): McKay, Davis and Fanning *Thoughts & Feelings*
Other therapies
  Timothy Gordon, Jessica Borushok , et al. *The ACT Approach*
  Matthew McKay, Jeffrey C. Wood, et al. *The Dialectical Behavior Therapy Skills Workbook*
  Francine Shapiro and Margot Silk, EMDR: *The Breakthrough Therapy for Overcoming Anxiety, Stress, and Trauma*
  Bessel van der Kolk, *The Body Keeps the Score*
  Mike Moreland, *EFT Tapping: Quick and Simple Exercises to De-Stress, Re-Energize and Overcome Emotional Problems Using Emotional Freedom Technique*

Workshops
Chestnut Paes Enneagram Academy
  www.mundoeneagrama.com/calendar
Riso-Hudson Certified and Authorized Teachers
  www.enneagraminstitute.com/workshops
Integrative Enneagram Solutions
  www.integrative9.com/events
Helen Palmer Workshops
  www.enneagram.com/teaching_schedule.html
The Narrative Enneagram
  enneagramworldwide.com/programs/
International Enneagram Association
  www.internationalenneagram.org/find-a/professional

Get in Contact
Comments or questions? Did you find any errors (let's not debate the use of the Oxford comma) or interested in forming a study group? You can email EnneagramJenn@gmail.com

Printed in Great Britain
by Amazon

42046825R00106